To Love God!

With All Your Heart, Soul and Might!

Compiled mostly from several pre-existing Booklets

First Printing - 2021

Revised for Second Printing - 2024

Published by "To Love GOD!"

Printed in the U.S.A.

By M.C. Murphy

Preface

This book is intended to bring to the forefront of the reader's mind, things that we as Christians, all too often just accept, without really thinking about it. So that the reader will begin to examine in more depth, things we may have just taken for granted.

The first two Chapters are a good example.

Chapter one is "To Love GOD"

This Chapter points out some very basic precepts, that are truly pivotal for each of us to truly, "To Love God" intensely and deeply.

Chapter two is "GOD So Loved The World"

In most Churches, we are frequently reminded that "GOD so loved the world that He gave His only begotten Son". This is usually repeated with some frequency in most Churches. Yet, most of us do not fully comprehend what this truly means. It means more than the average person recognizes or even understands.

If we stop and take the time to really think about what GOD did, by sending His Son to redeem mankind, then we need to take a much closer look at what is meant by:

The Redeemer and Redemption

> To Redeem = Recover, Reclaim, Retrieve, Repurchase, Buy back, Pay off, Restore, Buy off *or* Ransom.

To redeem something, it must be bought or bought back with something of equal or greater value. So, when GOD chose to redeem the children of Adam who would turn back to Him, the item's value, that was being used for the purchase needed to be, equal to or greater than, the value of the potential **total population**, of all who were being redeemed.

In order to Redeem those, of the children of Adam, who are **The Called Out Ones of GOD**. The value of the One being used to Redeem them, must out of necessity, **also** be **even more precious**, to **The Almighty**, than the **total** value of "**all**" those who are being Redeemed*!*

This book goes on, in the rest of the chapters, to address many common topics in a whole other light. Going into more depth than most people have ever taken the time to explore for themselves, up to this point. Hopefully, this will encourage the readers to take a more in-depth look into many things which up until now, most have just taken for granted, without taking the time to check them out for themselves. Whether in the various Church Doctrines or even in numerous different Bible Translations. This book intends to stimulate the reader's wish for a more in-depth desire for Bible study, as well as a more in-depth **understanding** and **closeness** to GOD*!*

With All Your Heart, Soul and Might !

Index

Chapter - 1	To Love God!	1
Chapter - 2	God So Loved The World	6
Chapter - 3	The Gospel of Christ !	12
Chapter - 4	My Father and I are One !	20
Chapter - 5	Co-Equal ?	25
Chapter - 6	The Word was God ?	31
Chapter - 7	Doubting Thomas	44
Chapter - 8	Is Jesus REALLY The Prince of Peace ?	48
Chapter - 9	The Government Will Be on His Shoulders	53
Chapter - 10	Immanuel and Righteous Branch	57
Chapter - 11	The First Commandment	62
Chapter - 12	The Curse of The Law	66
Chapter - 13	Temple Sacrifice	73
Chapter - 14	The Woman Caught in Adultery	80
Chapter - 15	How Should We View - The Law?	86
Chapter - 16	The New Covenant	92
Chapter - 17	The Sleep of Death	101
Addendum – 1	The Name (*of GOD*)	
Addendum – 2	The Levan of The Pharisee's	
Addendum – 3	Works	
Addendum – 4	The Law of Sin and Death	
Addendum – 5	Paul and The Law	
Addendum – 6	The Words of Paul	
Addendum – 7	Let Everything Be Established	

To Love GOD!

How do we know when we are actually loving GOD, and not just deceiving ourselves? By only giving lip service to the idea, all while falsely thinking that our declaration is proof enough for The Almighty. What is the difference between, deceiving ourselves and truly loving GOD. is when the central core of our **Life-Style** has become, (*to the best of our GOD given ability*) that we want to obey GOD and serve Him in everything that we do! Since, the central core of our **Life-Style**, has now become Obedience to GOD! As we said before; to the best of our GOD given ability. No matter how large or small that ability may be.

Yes, as we have just seen. We will endeavor to develop a **Life-Style** of Love, Devotion and Obedience to THE ALMIGHTY, to the very best of our GOD given ability! This is **NOT** something we cannot do! But rather, what we **can** do*!* If we truly Love GOD, then we will actually seek to do this!

By doing so, you will in effect, be seeking to **draw ever closer to Almighty GOD***!*

James 4:8 (NASB)
⁸ Draw **near to GOD** and He will draw near to you. Cleanse your hands, you sinners; and purify your hearts, you double-minded.

Deuteronomy 4:29 (NASB)
²⁹ But from there you will seek the LORD YOUR GOD, and you will find *Him* if you search for Him **with all your heart** and **all your soul**.

When you Love GOD and you obey and serve Him to the best of your ability, whenever you fall short because your ability was less than that which was needed to do the job. You will be forgiven! Because you will not be expected to do something that you cannot do! If you have also properly repented of your earlier willful disobedient **Life-Style** and now serve GOD with all your heart, soul and might, to the best of your GOD given ability, you will also in addition be forgiven for your old prior dis-obedient **Life-Style**, as well. Some claim that we are pre-forgiven. How have you been pre-forgiven? The forgiveness is there for you from the day you are born – **IF** you are willing to reach for it. By willfully choosing a **GODLY Life-Style.** Drawing near to GOD and serving Him, with **all your heart**, **all your soul**, **all your mind** and **all your strength**.

Ezekiel 33:12-19 (NASB)
¹² And you, **SON OF MAN**, say to your fellow citizens, 'The righteousness of a righteous man will **not** deliver him in the day of his transgression, and as for the wickedness of the wicked, he will **not** stumble because of it in the day when he turns (*repents*) from his

wickedness; whereas a righteous man will **not** be able to live (*Eternal Life*) by his righteousness on the day when he (*willfully*) commits sin.'

¹³ When I say to the righteous, he will surely live (*Eternal Life*), and he *so* trusts in his righteousness that he (*willfully*) commits iniquity, none of his righteous deeds **will be remembered**; but in that same iniquity of his which he has committed, he will die (*The Second Death – in the book of Revelation*).

¹⁴ But when I say to the wicked, 'You will surely die (*The Second Death*),' and he turns (*repents*) from his sin and practices justice and righteousness,

¹⁵ *if a* wicked man restores a pledge, pays back what he has taken by robbery, walks by the statutes which ensure life without committing iniquity, he shall surely live (*Eternal Life*); he shall **not** die (*The Second Death*).

¹⁶ None of his sins that he has committed will be remembered against him. He has practiced justice and righteousness; he shall surely live (*Eternal Life*).

¹⁷ "Yet your fellow citizens say, 'The way of the Lᴏʀᴅ is **not** right,' when it is their own way that is **not** right.

¹⁸ When the righteous turns from his righteousness and commits (*willful*) iniquity, then he shall die in it (*The Second Death*).

¹⁹ But when the wicked turns (*repents*) from his wickedness and practices justice and righteousness, he will live by them (*Eternal Life*).

Matthew 7:21-23 (NASB)

²¹ "Not everyone who says to Me, '**Lord, Lord,**'
will enter **The Kingdom of Heaven**,
but he who does the will of My Father who is in heaven *will enter*.

²² Many will say to Me on that day, '**Lord, Lord,**
did we not prophesy in **Your Name**,
and in **Your Name** cast out demons,
and in **Your Name** perform many miracles?'

²³ And then I will declare to them, 'I never knew you; ᴅᴇᴘᴀʀᴛ ꜰʀᴏᴍ Mᴇ, ʏᴏᴜ ᴡʜᴏ ᴘʀᴀᴄᴛɪᴄᴇ Lᴀᴡʟᴇꜱꜱɴᴇꜱꜱ.'

They appear to have been **un**-willing to do the will of the Heavenly Father, to the best of their Gᴏᴅ given ability! Instead, they excused their (*willful*) Lawless **Life-Style** (*of iniquity*), because they believed in Jesus and His love. They thought, that just because they believed in Jesus, that was enough? It appears that they may have been believing in a Different Jesus? One who did not put the Heavenly Father and His will above Himself*!* A Counterfeit Jesus? Whom they thought would except them even if they were practicing a (*willful*) Lawless **Life-Style** (*of iniquity*). One that did not put the will of the Heavenly Father first. They thought that as long as they accepted Jesus as Lord, that this would be enough.

Wrong ! ! !

Chapter 1 — To Love GOD!

The examples, in the Scripture Passages we saw earlier, show how a change in a person's **Life-Style** will alter what happens to them. When they stand before **The Almighty GOD** on the **Day of Judgment** and need for Jesus to intercede for them, as their **Advocate**, during this event.

What is it, that will enable us to **inherit Eternal Life**, when we stand before **Almighty GOD** on **The Day of Judgment**?

Luke 10:25-28 (NASB)

²⁵ And a lawyer stood up and put Him to the test, saying, "Teacher, what shall I do to **inherit Eternal Life**?"
²⁶ And He said to him, "What is written in the Law? How does it read to you?"
²⁷ And he answered, "YOU SHALL LOVE THE LORD YOUR GOD WITH ALL YOUR HEART, AND WITH ALL YOUR SOUL, AND WITH ALL YOUR STRENGTH, AND WITH ALL YOUR MIND; AND YOUR NEIGHBOR AS YOURSELF." (*Deut. 6:5 & Lev. 19:18*)
²⁸ And He said to him, "You have answered correctly; DO THIS AND YOU WILL LIVE."

Notice: Jesus agreed with this man! We see that if this is truly the central core of your own personal **Life-Style**. It will result in **inheriting** Eternal Life. Keep in mind, that an inheritance **cannot** be earned. But a **dis-obedient** Life-Style, can cause you to be **dis-inherited**. With your name being **blotted out** of the **Book of Life, where it once was**!

Psalm 69:28 (NASB)

²⁸ May they be **blotted out** of the book of life. And may they not be recorded with the righteous.

Exodus 32:33 (NASB)

³³ The LORD said to Moses, "Whoever has sinned against Me, I will **blot him out** of My book.

Revelation 3:5 (NKJV)

⁵ He who overcomes shall be clothed in white garments, and I will **not blot out** his name from **The Book of Life**; but I will confess his name before My Father and before His angels.

A very good example, of how GOD expects us to Love and Serve Him to the best of our GOD given ability, can be seen in the Parable of the Talents.

Matthew 25:14-30 (NASB)

¹⁴ "For *it is* just like a man *about* to go on a journey, who called his own slaves and entrusted his possessions to them.
¹⁵ To one he gave five talents, to another, two, and to another, one, each according to his own (*GOD given*) ability; and he went on his journey.

¹⁶ Immediately the one who had received the five talents went and traded with them, and gained five more talents.
¹⁷ In the same manner the one who *had received* the two *talents* gained two more.
¹⁸ But he who received the one *talent* went away, and dug *a hole* in the ground and hid his master's money.
¹⁹ "Now after a long time the master of those slaves came and settled accounts with them.
²⁰ The one who had received the five talents came up and brought five more talents, saying, 'Master, you entrusted five talents to me. See, I have gained five more talents.'
²¹ His master said to him, 'Well done, good and faithful slave. You were faithful with a few things; I will put you in charge of many things; enter into the joy of your master.'
²² "Also the one who *had received* the two talents came up and said, 'Master, you entrusted two talents to me. See, I have gained two more talents.'
²³ His master said to him, 'Well done, good and faithful slave. You were faithful with a few things; I will put you in charge of many things; enter into the joy of your master.'

²⁴ "And the one also who had received the one talent came up and said, 'Master, I knew you to be a hard man, reaping where you did not sow and gathering where you scattered no *seed*.
²⁵ And I was afraid, and went away and hid your talent in the ground. See, you have what is yours.'

²⁶ "But his master answered and said to him, 'You wicked, lazy slave, you knew that I reap where I did not sow and gather where I scattered no *seed*.
²⁷ Then you ought to have put my money in the bank, and on my arrival, I would have received my *money* back with interest.
²⁸ Therefore take away the talent from him, and give it to the one who has the ten talents.'

²⁹ "For to everyone who has, *more* shall be given, and he will have an abundance; but from the one who does not have, even what he does have shall be taken away.
³⁰ Throw out the worthless slave into the **outer darkness**; <u>in that place there will be **weeping** and **gnashing of teeth**</u>.

    Notice, that the one who only received One Talent was being punished, **not** for trying and failing! But rather, for **not** being even willing to try. (*To the best of his GOD given ability*.) Again, he is **not** being punished for trying and failing! But rather for being unwilling to even try. To the best of his GOD given ability, at all! Even if he had tried and failed, he probably would **not** have been cast out into <u>outer darkness</u>! **It is for being unwilling to even try, that he is being punished!**

> **Luke 13:23-28** (NASB)
> ²³ And someone said to Him, "Lord, are there *just* a few who are being saved?" And He said to them,
> ²⁴ "Strive to enter through the **narrow door**; for many, I tell you, will seek to enter and will **not** be able.
> ²⁵ Once the head of the house gets up and shuts the door, and you begin to stand outside and knock on the door, saying, 'LORD, open up to us!' then He will answer and say to you, 'I <u>do not</u> know where you are from.'
> ²⁶ Then you will begin to say, 'We ate and drank in Your presence, and You taught in our streets';
> ²⁷ and He will say, '<u>I tell you</u>; I <u>do not</u> know where you are from; DEPART FROM ME, ALL YOU EVILDOERS.'
> ²⁸ In that place there will be <u>weeping</u> and <u>gnashing of teeth</u> when you see Abraham and Isaac and Jacob and all The Prophets in **The Kingdom of GOD**, but yourselves being thrown out.

We have seen that if someone truly Loves GOD with all their Heart, Soul, Mind and Strength? Then they will develop a **Life-Style**, which will always seek to serve GOD and be **<u>Obedient</u>** to His Laws and Commandments. To the best of their GOD given ability. This is not the case for those who only give lip service to The Almighty GOD, as well as His Son. Even though in many cases they do Love GOD, but only to a point. Having a form of GODliness, while loving themselves and this world more. In doing so, in many cases, they have essentially deceived themselves. Trying to excuse the fact that they are actually living a **Life-Style**, which scripture refers to as that of an **<u>Evildoer</u>**! Mistakenly thinking that they are now under **"Grace"**!

> The Biblical Definition For - The **"Grace"** of GOD
> (*5485*) - The divine influence upon the heart;
> and its reflection in the life (*of the individual*).
> Resulting in receiving Unmerited Favor.

(*from Strong's Concordance*)

So, as **"THIS CHAPTER"** is coming to an end.

The Question is:

What kind of **Life-Style**,

have you chosen for **Yourself** ? ? ? ? ? ?

God so Loved the World!

John 3:16-21 (NASB)
¹⁶ "For GOD so loved the world, that He gave His only begotten Son, that whoever believes in Him shall not perish, but have <u>Eternal Life</u>.
¹⁷ For GOD did not send the Son into the world to judge the world, but that the world might be saved through Him.
¹⁸ He who believes in Him is not judged; he who does not believe has been judged already because he has not believed in the name of the only begotten Son of GOD.
¹⁹ This is the judgment, that the Light has come into the world, and men loved the darkness rather than the Light, for their deeds were evil.
²⁰ For everyone who does evil hates the Light and does not come to the Light for fear that his deeds will be exposed.
²¹ But he who practices the truth comes to the Light, so that his deeds may be manifested as having been wrought in GOD."

Let's take a close and careful look at what we have just read.

John 3:16-21 (NASB)
¹⁶ "For GOD so loved the world, that He gave His only begotten Son, that whoever believes in Him shall not perish, but have <u>Eternal Life</u>.

We see here that the **Heavenly Father** is using **His Son** as a tool, to present an opportunity of receiving <u>Eternal Life</u>, to those who are living in the world.

¹⁷ For GOD did not <u>send</u> the Son into the world to judge the world, but that the world might be saved through Him.

The **Heavenly Father** does not want to be compelled, to judge the world. **He** truly would rather for all of humanity, in this world, to turn to **Him** and **His Son**. In a right and proper manner, in order to be saved.

¹⁸ He who believes in Him is not judged; he who does not believe has been judged already because he has not believed in the name of the only begotten Son of GOD.

The word believes as it is used here, means to both believe and obey! So, to truly believe, in the manner that is being stated here you must be <u>obeying</u> **ALMIGHTY GOD,** as **HIS SON** is showing us here in John 3:18. Which is being elaborated on further, in James 2:17-20.

James 2:17-20 (NASB)
¹⁷ Even so faith (*belief*), if it has no works (*of obedience*), is dead, *being* by itself.
¹⁸ But someone may *well* say,
"You have faith (*belief*) and I have works (*of obedience*);
show me your faith (*belief*) without the works (*of obedience*),
and I will show you my faith (*belief*) by my works (*of obedience*)."

> ¹⁹ You believe that GOD is one. You do well; the demons also believe, and shudder.
> ²⁰ But are you willing to recognize, you foolish fellow, that faith (*belief*) without works (*of obedience*) is useless?

So, to truly believe in the manner that is being stated here. We must be obeying **ALMIGHTY GOD**. To the very best of our GOD given ability. At whatever our level of ability might be.

> ¹⁹ This is the judgment, that the Light has come into the world, and men loved the darkness rather than the Light, for their deeds were evil.
> ²⁰ For everyone who does evil hates the Light and does not come to the Light for fear that his deeds (*of dis-obedience*) will be exposed.
> ²¹ But he who practices the truth (*obedience*) comes to the Light, so that his deeds (*of obedience*) may be manifested as having been wrought in GOD."

Do not forget, what we read in chapter one, of this Book!

Matthew 7:21-23 (NASB)

> ²¹ "Not everyone who says to Me, '**Lord, Lord,**' will enter **The Kingdom of Heaven**, but he who does the will of My Father who is in heaven *will enter*.
> ²² Many will say to Me on that day, '**Lord, Lord**, did we not prophesy in **Your Name** (*Jesus*), and in **Your Name** (*Jesus*) cast out demons, and in **Your Name** (*Jesus*) perform many miracles?'
> ²³ And then I will declare to them, 'I never knew you; DEPART FROM ME, YOU WHO PRACTICE **LAWLESSNESS**.' (*Dis-obedience*)

Notice: That **Jesus** (*Yeshua*) puts **His Heavenly Father** and **His Father's will**, in a higher position of authority and importance than **Himself** or **His Own Name**!

Many people tend to forget or at least overlook that it was **not Jesus's idea**, for **Him** to redeem the children of Adam, after the fall of mankind!

It was **ALMIGHTY GOD** the **HEAVENLY FATHER'S** idea!

John 6:38 (NASB)

> ³⁸ For I have come down from heaven, **not** to do My own will, but the will of Him who sent Me.

John 5:30 (NASB)

> ³⁰ "I can do nothing on My own initiative. As I hear, I judge; and My judgment is just, because I do **not** seek My own will, but the will of Him who sent Me.

John 7:28-29 (NASB)

²⁸ Then Jesus cried out in the temple, teaching and saying, "You both know Me and know where I am from; and <u>I have not come of Myself</u>, but **He who sent Me is true**, whom you do not know. ²⁹ I know Him, because I am from Him, and **He sent Me**."

John 8:28 (NASB)

²⁸ So Jesus said, "When you lift up the Son of Man, then you will know that I am *He*, and <u>**I do nothing on My own initiative**</u>, but <u>I speak these things as the Father taught Me</u>.

John 8:42 (NASB)

⁴² Jesus said to them, "If GOD were your Father, you would love Me, for I proceeded forth and have come from GOD, <u>**for I have not even come on My own initiative**</u>, but <u>**He sent Me**</u>.

John 12:49 (NASB)

⁴⁹ For I did **not** speak <u>**on My own initiative**</u>, but the Father Himself <u>**who sent Me**</u> has given Me a commandment *as to* what to say and what to speak.

John 14:10 (NASB)

¹⁰ Do you not believe that I am in the Father, and the Father is in Me? The words that I say to you I do **not** speak <u>**on My own initiative**</u>, but the Father abiding in Me does His works.

In the next passage of Scripture, we see one place where **Jesus** (*Yeshua*) does use **His** Own Initiative. However, at the end of the passage, we see that even this was given to **Him** by **His Heavenly Father**.

John 10:17-18 (NASB)

¹⁷ For this reason the Father loves Me, because <u>I lay down My life so that I may take it again</u>.
¹⁸ <u>No one has taken it away from Me</u>, but <u>**I lay it down on My own initiative**</u>. <u>I have authority to lay it down</u>, and <u>I have authority to take it up again</u>. <u>This commandment I received from **My Father**</u>."

In the following three Scripture quotes from the New Testament, we see that the love **Jesus** (*Yeshua*) had for mankind, by its self, may not have been enough for Him to be willing to go through what lay before **Him**. It was only through **His** love **for His HEAVENLY FATHER** that **He** was able to go ahead and endure that which **He** knew was instore for **Him**. Remember, it was **NOT Jesus's idea** for **Him** to come and offer **Redemption** to mankind. It was **ALMIGHTY GOD** the **HEAVENLY FATHER'S** idea*!* And **Jesus** loved **Him** enough, that **He** was willing to do what **His HEAVENLY FATHER** had asked **Him** to do*!*

Matthew 26:39 (NASB)

³⁹ And He went a little beyond *them*, and fell on His face and prayed, saying, "My Father, if it is possible, let this cup pass from Me; <u>**yet not as I will, but as You will**</u>."

> **Mark 14:36** (NASB)
> ³⁶ And He was saying, "Abba! Father! All things are possible for You; remove this cup from Me; yet <u>not what I will</u>, <u>but what You will</u>."

> **Luke 22:41-44** (NASB)
> ⁴¹ And He withdrew from them about a stone's throw, and He knelt down and *began* to pray,
> ⁴² saying, "Father, if You are willing, remove this cup from Me; yet <u>not My will</u>, <u>but Yours be done</u>."
> ⁴³ Now an angel from heaven appeared to Him, strengthening Him.
> ⁴⁴ And being in agony He was praying very fervently; and His sweat became like drops of blood, falling down upon the ground.

Even though it appears that **Jesus** might have been, at this point, willing to let all of humanity remain un-redeemed, <u>by asking for this cup to pass from</u> **Him**, if it were left up to **Jesus**. Nevertheless, because the <u>Redemption</u> of mankind was <u>not His idea</u>, to begin with, but rather **His HEAVENLY FATHER'S** plan. It was for **His HEAVENLY FATHER**, that **Jesus** was willing to go ahead.

Remember; in John 3:16-21, it was The **ALMIGHTY'S** intention to <u>send</u> **His Son** to redeem the human inhabitants of Planet Earth. Because of the **HEAVENLY FATHER'S** love for all of the <u>descendants of Adam</u>.

> **Matthew 26:53-54** (NIV)
> ⁵³ Do you think I cannot call on **My Father**, and **He** will at once put at my disposal more than twelve legions of angels? (*more than 72,000 angels*)
> ⁵⁴ But how then would the <u>Scriptures be fulfilled</u> that say it <u>must</u> happen in this way?"

It appears that **Jesus** was willing to go ahead and go through with the **Redemption** of mankind. Not only for the sake of just humanity! But, because He loved **ALMIGHTY GOD** with <u>**All** His heart</u>, <u>**All** His mind</u>, <u>**All** His soul</u> and <u>**All** His strength</u>! And it was for **Him**, **His HEAVENLY FATHER** that **He** was willing to go through with the **Redemption** of mankind! As Jesus declares to **His HEAVENLY FATHER**, "<u>not</u> <u>My will</u>, <u>but Your will</u>, <u>be done</u>!" Knowing, **The FATHER** had <u>sent</u> **Him** to redeem mankind! (*John 3:16*)

> **Mark 12:28-34** (NASB)
> ²⁸ One of the scribes came and heard them arguing, and recognizing that He had answered them well, asked Him, **"What commandment is the foremost of all?"**
> ²⁹ Jesus answered, "The foremost is, 'HEAR, O ISRAEL! THE LORD OUR GOD IS ONE LORD;
> ³⁰ AND YOU SHALL LOVE THE LORD YOUR GOD WITH ==ALL YOUR HEART, AND WITH ALL YOUR SOUL, AND WITH ALL YOUR MIND, AND WITH ALL YOUR STRENGTH==.' (*Deut. 6:4-5*)

³¹ The second is this, '**YOU SHALL LOVE YOUR NEIGHBOR AS YOURSELF**.' (*Lev. 19:18*) There is no other commandment greater than these."
³² The scribe said to Him, "Right, Teacher; You have truly stated that **HE IS ONE, AND THERE IS NO ONE ELSE BESIDES HIM;**
³³ **AND TO LOVE HIM** WITH **ALL THE HEART** AND WITH **ALL THE UNDERSTANDING** AND WITH **ALL THE STRENGTH, AND TO LOVE ONE'S NEIGHBOR AS HIMSELF**, is much more than all burnt offerings and sacrifices."
³⁴ When Jesus saw that he had answered intelligently, He said to him, "You are not far from **The Kingdom of GOD**." After that, no one would venture to ask Him any more questions.

1 Samuel 15:22 (NASB)

²² Samuel said,
"Has the LORD as much delight in burnt offerings and sacrifices
   As in obeying the voice of the LORD?
Behold, to obey **is better** than sacrifice,
And to **heed** than the fat of rams.

Let's take another look at the verses from earlier in this chapter, that are also in chapter one, Matthew 7:21-23, as well as reviewing, Luke 10:25-28 that is also from chapter one.

Matthew 7:21-23 (NASB)

²¹ "Not everyone who says to Me, '**Lord, Lord**,' will enter **The Kingdom of Heaven**, but he who does the WILL of My Father who is in heaven *will enter*.
²² Many will say to Me on that day, '**Lord, Lord**, did we not prophesy in **Your Name** (*Jesus*), and in **Your Name** (*Jesus*) cast out demons, and in **Your Name** (*Jesus*) perform many miracles?'
²³ And then I will declare to them, 'I never knew you; DEPART FROM ME, YOU WHO PRACTICE **LAWLESSNESS**.' (*Dis-obedience*)

Luke 10:25-28 (NASB)

²⁵ And a lawyer stood up and put Him to the test, saying, "Teacher, what shall I do to **inherit Eternal Life**?"
²⁶ And He said to him, "What is written in the Law? How does it read to you?"
²⁷ And he answered, "**YOU SHALL LOVE THE LORD YOUR GOD WITH ALL YOUR HEART, AND WITH ALL YOUR SOUL, AND WITH ALL YOUR STRENGTH, AND WITH ALL YOUR MIND; AND YOUR NEIGHBOR AS YOURSELF.**" (*Deut. 6:5 & Lev. 19:18*)
²⁸ And He said to him, "You have answered correctly; DO THIS AND YOU WILL LIVE.

Do you believe that when Jesus, in effect, told the Lawyer: "If he wanted to inherit Eternal Life, that he would need to make loving GOD First, with all his heart, soul, strength and mind.   Second after that, to then love his neighbor as himself." This was to be at the very central core, of his (*the Lawyer's*) own personal Life-Style!

If so, then the question is:

What is at the central core

of your own,

personal Life-Style ? ? ? ? ? ? ? ? ?

The Gospel of Christ!

The **Apostles Creed** is the abbreviated form of the **Gospel of Christ**, used in many Churches.

> I believe in GOD the Father Almighty, maker of heaven and earth; and in Jesus Christ, his only Son, our Lord, who was conceived by the Holy Spirit, born of the Virgin Mary, suffered under Pontius Pilate, was crucified, died, and was buried; he descended to the dead. On the third day, he rose again; he ascended into heaven, is seated at the right hand of the Father, and will come again to judge the living and the dead. I believe in the Holy Spirit, the holy catholic church, the communion of saints, the forgiveness of sins, the resurrection of the body, and the life everlasting. Amen.

This abbreviated Gospel conveniently overlooks the **entire ministry of Jesus**. As though it was **not** important enough, to even mention*!*

Even in the Churches that do not use the **Apostles Creed** in their worship. Usually say that the Gospel is the story of **The Life of Jesus**. Calling the first four books of the New Testament, The Fore Gospels. Because they are the stories of **The Life of Jesus**. Even so, they usually overlook the very thing which Jesus said, was actually (*The Fullness of*) **The Gospel**, that He was so fervently preaching.

What was the Gospel that **Jesus** (*Yeshua*) **preached**, throughout His earthly ministry?

Mark 1:14 (NASB)
¹⁴ Now after John had been taken into custody, Jesus came into Galilee, preaching **The Gospel of GOD**,
¹⁵ and saying, "The time is fulfilled, and **The Kingdom of GOD** is at hand; repent and believe in **The Gospel**."

What was this, Gospel? It was "The Gospel of GOD" – "The Gospel of GOD's Kingdom"*!*

Jesus was **not** preaching the abbreviated "Gospel of Jesus Christ" preached in most Churches today. Which is only a portion or piece of "The Gospel of The Kingdom of God"*!*

Matthew 4:23 (NASB)
²³ Jesus was going throughout all Galilee, teaching in their synagogues and proclaiming **The Gospel of The Kingdom**, and healing every kind of disease and every kind of sickness among the people.

Matthew 9:35 (NASB)
³⁵ Jesus was going through all the cities and villages, teaching in their synagogues and proclaiming **The Gospel of The Kingdom**, and healing every kind of disease and every kind of sickness.

Matthew 24:14 (NASB)
¹⁴ This **Gospel of The Kingdom** shall be preached in the whole world as a testimony to all the nations, and then the end will come.

Jesus is **not** saying, it is **_only_** the Gospel of Jesus or the Gospel of Christ! But rather, it is **The Gospel of The Kingdom of GOD**, also known as **The Gospel of The Kingdom of Heaven**! Jesus speaks many times about this. He even gives analogies about **The Kingdom of Heaven** in the form of parables, time and again. One of these is the parable of a man who sows good seed.

Matthew 13:24-30 (NASB)

24 Jesus presented another parable to them, saying, "**The Kingdom of Heaven** may be compared to a man who sowed good seed in his field.
25 But while his men were sleeping, his enemy came and sowed tares among the wheat and went away.
26 But when the wheat sprouted and bore grain, then the tares became evident also.
27 The slaves of the landowner came and said to him, 'Sir, did you not sow good seed in your field? How then does it have tares?'
28 And he said to them, 'An enemy has done this!' The slaves said to him, 'Do you want us, then, to go and gather them up?'
29 But he said, 'No; for while you are gathering up the tares, you may uproot the wheat with them.
30 Allow both to grow together until the harvest; and in the time of the harvest, I will say to the reapers, "First gather up the tares and bind them in bundles to burn them up; but gather the wheat into my barn."'"

Today in many, if not most, of the Churches we see Ministers, Pastors and Evangelists frequently preaching and teaching something to the effect that, "It is impossible to **keep** the **Old Testament Law**!" They go on to frequently claim, the only reason that GOD gave **The Law** was to prove that **No One** can keep them! However, they overlook that **The Kingdom of GOD** and **His Government** are based on and ruled by **GOD's Laws**! Are they then, the wheat or the tares?

What did **GOD** have to say about a person's ability to keep **His Laws**?

Deuteronomy 30:11 (NIV)
11 Now what I am commanding you today is **not** too difficult for you
or beyond your reach.

GOD even gives us examples in Scripture of people who took GOD at His Word and went about doing what GOD told them to do!

Genesis 26:5 (NASB)
5 because Abraham obeyed Me and kept My Charge,
My Commandments, My Statutes and **My Laws**."

Notice: The Commandments, Statutes and Laws of GOD, were already in effect. They were known and observed by Abraham. Hundreds of years before Moses and the events that occurred at Sinai! The Levitical priesthood was only implemented after the disaster with the Golden Calf. Because up until then, it had been the obligation of the (*first begotten*) first-born male child, that had opened the womb, was the one who was to be a priest (*after the order of Melchizedek*).

Luke 1:5-6 (NASB)
5 In the days of Herod, king of Judea, there was a priest named **Zacharias**, of the division of Abijah; and he had a wife from the daughters of Aaron, and her name was **Elizabeth**.

⁶ They were both righteous in the sight of GOD, **walking blamelessly in all** the Commandments and Requirements of **The LORD**.

Levites and especially the Priest who were of the line of Aaron, had far more requirements placed on them in **GOD'S LAWS**, than the average person. Yet, Zacharias and Elizabeth were blameless when it came to keeping, not only, The Laws and Commandments required of the average person. But they were also blameless, when it came to keeping all of the other Laws and Commandments that were unique to the descendants of Aaron. Again, this was far more than was required of the average person! And yet, they were able to do what **GOD** expected of them!

Those of us who are just average individuals are required to do less! You may say, well I am not a descendant of Abraham, Isaac and Jacob. So, how would this apply to me?

The answer is: that time and again, in varying ways, **GOD** tells us, that He intends that there is to be ONLY ONE **LAW**, for both Jew and Gentiles, for the children of Abraham, Isaac and Jacob and for those of all the other Nations on earth.

Deuteronomy 29:10-15 (NASB)

¹⁰ "You stand today, all of you, before the LORD your GOD: your chiefs, your tribes, your elders and your officers, *even* all the men of Israel,
¹¹ your little ones, your wives, and the ALIEN who is within your camps, from the one who chops your wood to the one who draws your water,
¹² that you (*which includes these Aliens*) may enter into the covenant with the LORD your GOD, and into His oath which the LORD your GOD is making with you today,
¹³ in order that He may establish you today as His people and that He may be your GOD, just as He spoke to you and as He swore to your fathers, to Abraham, Isaac, and Jacob.
¹⁴ **"Now not with you alone am I making this covenant and this oath,**
¹⁵ **but both with those who stand here with us today in the presence of the LORD our GOD and with those who are not with us here today."**

Since all of Israel and the Aliens of the Mixed Multitude (*Gentiles*) who left Egypt with the Children of Israel are there to enter into the Covenant with the **Lord GOD**. The others who are **not** there with them that day would be all the other descendants of Adam. The rest of the Nations of the Earth, which would be the rest of the **Gentiles**.

Exodus 12:47-49 (NKJV)

⁴⁷ "All the congregation of Israel shall keep it.
⁴⁸ And when a **STRANGER** dwells with you *and wants* to keep the Passover to the LORD, let all his males be circumcised, and then let him come near and keep it; and **he shall be as a native of the land**. For no uncircumcised person shall eat it.
⁴⁹ **ONE LAW shall be for the native-born** and for the **STRANGER who dwells among you**."

Leviticus 24:21-22 (NKJV)

²¹ "And whoever kills an animal shall restore it; but whoever kills a man shall be put to death.
²² **You shall have the same Law for the STRANGER and for one from your own country**; for I *am* the LORD your GOD."

Numbers 15:14-16 (NASB)

¹⁴ "If an ALIEN sojourns with you, or one who may be among you throughout your generations, **and he *wishes to* make an offering by fire, as a soothing aroma to the LORD, just as you do so he shall do**.
¹⁵ *As for* the assembly, **there shall be one statute for you and for the ALIEN who sojourns *with you*, a perpetual statute throughout your generations; as you are, so shall the ALIEN be before the LORD**.
¹⁶ **There is to be ONE LAW AND ONE ORDINANCE for you and for the ALIEN who sojourns with you**."

Notice - at the end of verse fifteen it says:

"**as you are, so shall the ALIEN be before the LORD**"

Numbers 19:10 (NKJV)

¹⁰ And the one who gathers the ashes of the heifer shall wash his clothes and be unclean until evening. **It shall be a statute forever to the children of Israel and to the STRANGER who dwells among them.**

Deuteronomy 27:19 (NASB)

¹⁹ "**Cursed is he who distorts the justice** due an ALIEN, orphan, and widow." And all the people shall say, "Amen."

Isaiah 11:1-4, 10 (NIV)

¹ A SHOOT will come up **from the stump of Jesse**;
from his roots a Branch will bear fruit.
² The Spirit of the LORD will rest on him -
the Spirit of wisdom and of understanding,
the Spirit of counsel and of power,
the Spirit of knowledge and of the fear of the LORD –
³ and he will delight in the fear of the LORD.
He will not judge by what he sees with his eyes,
or decide by what he hears with his ears;
⁴ but with righteousness he will judge the needy,
with justice, he will give decisions for the poor of the earth. ...

¹⁰ In that day, the **ROOT of Jesse** will stand as a banner for the people;
the Nations (*the Gentiles*) will rally to him,
and his place of rest will be **Glorious**.

And to these Gentiles who will rally to **Him**, the **Root of Jesse** and to **His** place of rest, which is truly **Glorious**; to them and everyone else:

He declares the following:

Jesus said in
Matthew 5:17-19 (NASB)
¹⁷ "**Do not think** that I came to abolish **The Law** or **The Prophets**;
I did **not** come to abolish, but to fulfill.
¹⁸ For truly I say to you, until heaven and earth pass away,
not the smallest letter or stroke shall pass away from **The Law**,
until all is accomplished. (*In The Law and The Prophets, includes The Millenium*)
¹⁹ Whoever then annuls one of the least of these Commandments,
and so teaches others, shall be called least in **The Kingdom of Heaven**;
but whoever keeps and teaches them,
he shall be called great in **The Kingdom of Heaven**."

We know that all has **not** yet been accomplished, because the fulfillment of many prophecies including those of the Second Coming of Jesus, **have not yet occurred**! In spite of that, many Christians who declare Jesus as their Lord; say that Jesus did away with The Law! Perhaps whether consciously or sub-consciously, it is being done in order to justify the fact that their **Life-Style** is what scripture refers to as living in a **Law**less manner. While at the same time declaring Jesus to be their Lord and Savior**?**

Remember what we read, in earlier chapters*!*

Matthew 7:21-23 (NASB)
²¹ "Not everyone who says to Me, '**Lord, Lord,**' will enter **The Kingdom of Heaven**, but he who does the will of My Father who is in heaven *will enter*.
²² Many will say to Me on that day, '**Lord, Lord**, did we not prophesy in **Your Name** (*Jesus*), and in **Your Name** (*Jesus*) cast out demons, and in **Your Name** (*Jesus*) perform many miracles?'
²³ And then I will declare to them, 'I never knew you; DEPART FROM ME, YOU WHO PRACTICE **LAWLESSNESS**.' (*Dis-obedience*)

Once again, how do we know when we are actually loving **GOD** and not deceiving ourselves by only giving lip service to the idea? Thinking that our declaration is proof enough. The difference between, deceiving ourselves and truly loving **GOD**, is when the central core of our **Life-Style** has become, (*to the best of our GOD given ability, without turning back*) that we want to obey **GOD** and serve Him in everything that we do! The forgiveness of our sins and heartfelt Obedience, is to be the foundation of **THE GOSPEL OF GOD**, also known as **THE GOSPEL OF THE KINGDOM OF GOD**, or **THE GOSPEL OF THE KINGDOM OF HEAVEN**. After our forgiveness, we are expected and obligated to make the central core of our **Life-Style; Obedience** to **GOD***!* To the best of our **GOD** given ability. No matter how large or small that ability maybe. Without turning back to willful **Sin***!*

Yes, as we said before: We will endeavor to develop a **Life-Style** of **Love**, **Devotion** and **Obedience**, to **THE ALMIGHTY**, to the very best of our **GOD** given ability*!* This is **NOT** something we can-not do*!* But rather, what we **can** do*!* And if we truly Love **GOD**, we will **seek** to do this*!*

Deuteronomy 13:1-4 (NASB)
¹ "If a prophet or a dreamer of dreams arises among you and gives you
a sign or a wonder,

² and the sign or the wonder comes true, concerning which he spoke to you, saying, 'Let us go after other gods (whom you have not known) and let us serve them,'
³ you shall not listen to the words of that prophet or that dreamer of dreams; for the LORD your GOD is testing you to find out if you **love the LORD your GOD with <u>all your heart and with all your soul</u>.**
⁴ <u>You shall follow the LORD your GOD and fear Him</u>; and <u>you shall keep His Commandments</u>, <u>listen to His voice</u>, <u>serve Him</u>, and <u>cling to Him</u>.

During His ministry, we see several different passages in the New Testament, where Jesus was asked, which of the Commandments is the most important? When He answered, He also at times, mentioned how this relates to the **GOSPEL OF THE KINGDOM OF GOD**. This **Gospel** was the foundation upon which He based His ministry*!* Let us quickly review what we have already seen toward the end of Chapter Two.

Mark 12:28-34 (NASB)

²⁸ One of the scribes came and heard them arguing, and recognizing that He had answered them well, asked Him, **"What commandment is the foremost of all?"**
²⁹ Jesus answered, "The foremost is, 'HEAR, O ISRAEL! THE LORD OUR GOD IS ONE LORD;
³⁰ AND YOU SHALL LOVE THE LORD YOUR GOD WITH <u>ALL YOUR HEART</u>, AND WITH <u>ALL YOUR SOUL</u>, AND WITH <u>ALL YOUR MIND</u>, AND WITH <u>ALL YOUR STRENGTH</u>.' (*Deut.6:4-5*)
³¹ The second is this, (*Lev. 19:18*) '<u>YOU SHALL LOVE YOUR NEIGHBOR AS YOURSELF</u>.' There is no other commandment greater than these."
³² The scribe said to Him, "Right, Teacher; You have truly stated that **HE IS ONE, AND THERE IS NO ONE ELSE BESIDES HIM;**
³³ AND TO LOVE HIM WITH ALL THE HEART AND WITH ALL THE UNDERSTANDING AND WITH ALL THE STRENGTH, AND TO LOVE ONE'S NEIGHBOR AS HIMSELF, ==is much more than all burnt offerings and sacrifices==."
³⁴ When Jesus saw that he had answered intelligently, He said to him, "You are not far from **The Kingdom of GOD**." After that, no one would venture to ask Him any more questions.

1 Samuel 15:22 (NASB)

²² Samuel said,
"Has the LORD as much delight in burnt offerings and sacrifices
As in obeying the voice of the LORD?
Behold, ==to obey **is better** than sacrifice==,
And to **heed** than the fat of rams.

Psalm 51:15-17 (NASB)

¹⁵ Lord, open my lips, so that my mouth may declare Your praise.
¹⁶ For You ==do not delight in sacrifice==, otherwise I would give it; You ==do not take pleasure in burnt offerings==.
¹⁷ The ==sacrifices of GOD are a broken spirit; a broken and a contrite heart==, O God, You will **not** despise.

> **Micah 6:8** (NASB)
>
> ⁸ He has told you, mortal one, what is good; and what does the Lord require of you? But to <mark>do justice</mark>, to <mark>love kindness</mark>, and to <mark>walk humbly with your GOD</mark>!

> **Jeremiah 7:22-23** (NKJV)
>
> ²² For I did not speak to your fathers, or command them in the day that I brought them out of the land of Egypt, <mark>concerning burnt offerings or sacrifices.</mark>
> ²³ But this is what I commanded them, saying, '<mark>Obey My voice</mark>, and <mark>I will be your GOD</mark>, and <mark>you shall be My people</mark>. And walk in all the ways that I have commanded you, that it may be well with you.'

> **Hosea 6:6** (NASB)
>
> ⁶ For <mark>I desire **loyalty** rather than sacrifice</mark>, and <mark>**knowledge of GOD** rather than burnt offerings</mark>.

As we just read in, 1ˢᵗ Samuel, Psalms, Micah, Jeremiah and Hosea. This was nothing new! This attitude and desire that we see, of wanting to first <u>REPENT</u> of your **Sins**. Resulting then in the overwhelming desire to <u>Love</u>, <u>Serve</u> and <u>Obey</u> **ALMIGHTY GOD**. Was and still is, at the very <u>central core</u>, of the **GOSPEL OF THE KINGDOM OF GOD**. That was preached by **Jesus**, throughout His earthly ministry.

The Gospel of GOD also known as The Gospel of The Kingdom, includes the prophecies of The Messiah (*or Christ*). With the Gospel of The Kingdom showing how The Messiah (*or Christ*) will administer GOD's Kingdom, on this earth during The Millenium and throughout eternity when there is a New Heavens and a New Earth. When a church only speaks of The Messiah's (*or Christ's*) Death Burial and Resurrection, resulting in the forgiveness of Sins. As truly important as this actually is! It is still incomplete when it comes to understanding the full scope of the <u>**Government of God's Kingdom**</u> and how GOD's Laws will be used by **His Messiah** (*or Christ*).

> **Galatians 1:6-10** (NASB)
>
> ⁶ I am amazed that you are so quickly deserting Him who called you by the **grace** of Christ, for a different gospel, (*which does not require Obedience*)
>
> > The Biblical Definition For - The **"Grace"** of GOD
> > (*5485*) - The divine influence upon the heart
> > and its reflection in the life (*of the individual*).
> > Resulting in the receiving of unmerited favor from GOD.
>
> (*from Strong's Concordance*)
>
> > **"Grace"** does <u>**not**</u> mean **"forgiveness"**!
> > It is <u>**not**</u> a **"get out of Hell"** free card!
>
> ⁷ which is not *just* another *account*; but there are some who are disturbing you and want to distort the gospel of Christ.

⁸ But even if we, or an angel from heaven, should preach to you a gospel contrary to what we have preached to you, (*what was the Gospel that they preached*) he is to be accursed!
⁹ As we have said before, even now I say again: if anyone is preaching to you a gospel contrary to what you received, (*what was the Gospel that they received*) he is to be accursed!

Obviously, Paul was not referring to the **"Gospel of the Kingdom of God"** preached by **Jesus**? Otherwise, Paul would be saying that **Jesus**, was to be accursed*!*

Matthew 24:14 (NASB)
¹⁴ This **Gospel of The Kingdom** shall be preached in the whole world as a testimony to all the nations, and then the end will come.

It was that segment or portion, of the **"Gospel of the Kingdom of God"**, referred to as the **"Gospel of Christ"**, which some of the Galatians were perverting. Claiming that all they needed to do, was for them to say that they accept Jesus, as their Lord and Savior. In order to get the equivalent of a **"get out of Hell"** free card! Without being Obedient, to the best of their God given ability. Mistakenly thinking, that because of this declaration, that their continuing, ongoing and **willful**; **Lawless Life Style**, was now covered by **"The blood of Jesus"** (Not So Matthew 7:21-23).

"Not everyone who says to Me, 'Lord, Lord,' will enter The Kingdom of Heaven,…"

Matthew 7:21-23 is referring to **Obedience**, which is the Deep, Heart-Felt, Love and Devotion that is giving rise to that **Obedience**! Among those who are a part of **His Kingdom**!

To redeem something, it must be bought or bought back with something of equal or greater value. So, when GOD chose to redeem the children of Adam who would turn back to Him, the item's value, that was being used for the purchase needed to be, equal to or greater than, the value of the potential **total population**, of all who were being redeemed.

In order to Redeem those, of the children of Adam, who are **The Called Out Ones of GOD**. The value of the One being used to Redeem them, must out of necessity, **also** be **even more precious**, to **The Almighty**, than the total value of "**all**" those who are being Redeemed*!* God used for that payment, the Death of **Yeshua** (Jesus) **His Son**, on The Cross*!*

So, once again, the question is:

What is at the central core

of your own,

personal Life-Style ? ? ? ? ? ? ? ? ?

My Father and I are One!

Many times, people want to use this statement by Jesus as proof that Jesus is Almighty God, the Creator of the Universe and all that is in it.

The question is; When it says in the New Testament that Jesus and His Father are ONE, is it a plural One or a solitary One?

At this point, many are asking; "What in the world is a plural One?"

Some quick examples would be - One dozen Eggs, One platoon (*or squad*) of Soldiers, One fleet of Ships, One Family, and One Nation (*of people*) under God. All of these are just a few examples of plural Ones which are a number of things that are united to form a single group. Which shows that there is a degree of unity or One-ness. Such as when Scripture says that a Husband and Wife are One*!* It is quite obvious that a Husband and Wife are **not** the same person. Just as One Nation can-**not** be a single person.

So, when we see in Scripture that Jesus said in John 10:30 "I and the Father are One." With just a little Bible study, we can see that Jesus did **not** say that they are the same person*!*

One such example, which shows us that Jesus and His Heavenly Father are not the same person, is when we see Jesus being baptized in the Jordan River by John the Baptist.

Mark 1:9-11 (NIV)

> [9] At that time Jesus came from Nazareth in Galilee and was baptized by John in the Jordan.
> [10] As Jesus was coming up out of the water, he saw heaven being torn open and the Spirit descending on him like a dove.
> [11] And a voice came from heaven: "You are my Son, Whom I love; with you I am well pleased."

Jesus is **not** being a ventriloquist and saying this about Himself*!*

In addition, we have a later example when we see that Jesus is asking God to bless His followers in the book of John chapter 17 verse 22 (NASB) "…that they may be One, just as We are One". Jesus asked in His prayer to Almighty God that He (*Jesus*) wanted these people to be One just as He and His Father were One. Whether you take His prayer as meaning that He wanted them all to be One with the Almighty Heavenly Father just as He was? Or, if you take it the other way, as though He wanted them to be One with each other. Just as He and His Father were One. No matter which way you may choose to take it. The words of Jesus's prayer give an example. This shows that for them to be One as Jesus and the Father are One would require that Jesus and His Father are separate and distinct beings. Jesus went on to explain further in the very next two passages of John chapter 17 verses 23 through 24 (NASB). "I in them, and Thou in Me, that they may be perfected in unity, that the world may know that Thou didst send Me, and didst love them, even as Thou didst love Me. Father, I desire that they also, whom Thou hast given Me, be with

Me where I am, in order that they may behold My glory, which Thou hast given Me; for Thou didst love Me before the foundation of the world." Just as the people for whom the prayer is being said are separate entities and are separate from Jesus! It shows that Jesus and His Father are not the same person just as the believers for whom He is praying are not the same entity as Jesus! So, being One with Jesus does **not** make you Jesus, any more than Jesus being One with Almighty God would make Jesus, God. For if it did, then all of these believers would also be God! Because being One with Jesus, they thereby would also be One with God, so they would also be Gods.

John 10:22-42 (NASB)

22 At that time the Feast of the Dedication took place at Jerusalem;

23 it was winter, and Jesus was walking in the temple in the portico of Solomon.

24 The Jews therefore gathered around Him, and were saying to Him, "How long will You keep us in suspense? If You are the Christ, tell us plainly."

25 Jesus answered them, "I told you, and you do not believe; the works that I do in My Father's name, these bear witness of Me."

26 "But you do not believe, because you are not of My sheep."

27 "My sheep hear My voice, and I know them, and they follow Me;

28 and I give **Eternal Life** to them, and they shall never perish; and no One shall snatch them out of My hand."

29 "My Father, who has given *them* to Me, is greater than all; and no One is able to snatch *them* out of the Father's hand."

30 "I and the Father are One."

31 The Jews took up stones again to stone Him.

32 Jesus answered them, "I showed you many good works from the Father; for which of them are you stoning Me?"

33 The Jews answered Him, "For a good work we do not stone You, but for blasphemy; and because You, being a man, make Yourself out *to be* God."

34 Jesus answered them, "Has it not been written in your Law, 'I SAID, YOU ARE GODS'?" (Ps. 82:6-7)

35 "If he called them gods, to whom the word of God came (and the Scripture cannot be broken),

36 do you say of Him, whom the Father sanctified and sent into the world, 'You are blaspheming,' because I said. 'I am the Son of God'?

37 "If I do not do the works of My Father, do not believe Me;

38 but if I do them, though you do not believe Me, believe the works, that you may know and understand that the Father is in Me, and I in the Father."

39 Therefore, they were seeking again to seize Him, and He eluded their grasp.

40 And He went away again beyond the Jordan to the place where John was first baptizing, and He was staying there.

41 And many came to Him and were saying, "While John performed no sign, yet everything John said about this man was true."

42 And many believed in Him there.

Many people are confused when they read the statement that Jesus made in John chapter ten verse thirty-eight.

> **38** but if I do them, though you do not believe Me, believe the works, that you may know and understand that the Father is in Me, and I in the Father."

In the physical realm, a portion of the human father is in his son and a portion of his son is in his father. Because part of a human father's genome is in his son and a portion of his human son's genome is still in his human father. Yet, they are not the same person!

In the spiritual realm, a portion of the heavenly Father is in His Son and a portion of the Son is in His Father. Because part of the heavenly Father's spirit is in His Son and a portion of His Son's spiritual essence is also still in His Heavenly Father. Yet, they are not the same person!

It is then no surprise when Jesus then says in John chapter ten and verse thirty.

30 "I and the Father are One."

It is because they are of One heart, One mind, One spirit, and One purpose. In all things even when it comes to including what God has offered to mankind. And that is why Jesus later asked His Heavenly Father the following.

John 17:11 (NIV)
11 "… so that they may be One as we are One."

John 17:22 (NIV)
22 "… that they may be One as we are One."

Jesus is asking His Heavenly Father to grant those who believed that He (*Jesus*) was the Messiah and the Son of God, to be given a divine blessing. So that they would be of - One heart, One mind, One spirit and One purpose. To become One with God (*just as Jesus was*) and by default also to be One with each other. Because Jesus wants these individuals for whom He is praying, to truly love the Lord God of Heaven, with **all** their hearts, with **all** their souls, with **all** their minds and with **all** that they possess.

Jesus never, I repeat never, claimed that He (*Jesus*) was יהוה Yehovah (*Jehovah*), the One who is called Jehovah in English. Because יהוה Yehovah (*Jehovah*) is a single solitary entity! In Deuteronomy chapter six, He is the One of whom the Shema is declaring the following:

Deuteronomy 6:4-5
"Hear, Oh Israel, יהוה Yehovah (*Jehovah*) is our God, יהוה Yehovah (*Jehovah*) is One. You shall love יהוה Yehovah (*Jehovah*) your God with all your heart, with all your soul, and with all your might, …"

However, Jesus does declare that He is THE SON OF GOD! What does this mean? When you understand that a **Son** is the offspring or creation of His parent! Then you will realize that Jesus is declaring that Almighty God created Him! Yes, Jesus is saying that He is the offspring, the creation, of **The Heavenly Father**!

John 17:24 (NIV)

²⁴ "Father, I want those you have given me to be with me where I am, and to see my glory, the glory you have given me because you loved me before the **Creation of The World**."

Colossians 1:15 (NIV)

¹⁵ The Son is the image of the invisible God, the **firstborn** over **All Creation**.

Proverbs 8:22-31 (NIV)

²² "The LORD brought me forth as the first of His works, before His deeds of old;
²³ I was appointed from eternity, from the beginning, **before the world began**.
²⁴ When there were no oceans, **I was given birth**, when there were no springs abounding with water;
²⁵ before the mountains were settled in place, before the hills, **I was given birth**,
²⁶ before He made the earth or its fields or any of the dust of the world.
²⁷ I was there when He set the heavens in place, when He marked out the horizon on the face of the deep,
²⁸ when He established the clouds above and fixed securely the fountains of the deep,
²⁹ when He gave the sea its boundary so the waters would not overstep his command, and when He marked out the foundations of the earth.
³⁰ Then I was the craftsman **at His side**. I was filled with delight day after day, rejoicing always in His presence,
³¹ rejoicing in His whole world and delighting in mankind."

> The Book of Proverbs is a collection of unrelated proverbs, assembled into a single book. To show where one proverb stops and the next begins, the Hebrew codex used for translating most of the English versions of the Bible, has the Hebrew letter ס placed at the end of a proverbial section to indicate where one stops and the other starts. Proverbs chapter eight has a ס at the end of verse 21 (*just before the beginning of verse 22*) and at the end of verse 31. Showing that it is un-connected and un-related to the proverbs both before it and after it!

Once again Jesus never, I repeat never, claimed that He (*Jesus*) was יהוה Yehovah (*Jehovah*), the One who in English is called Jehovah. Because Yehovah (*Jehovah*) יהוה is a single solitary entity! Yehovah (*Jehovah*) יהוה who is THE **ALMIGHTY HEAVENLY FATHER**, is the ONE who brought Him (*Jesus*) forth into existence before the world began! Before, even the heavens were set in place! He was already at the side of **THE ALMIGHTY GOD OF CREATION** before this Realm or Physical Dimension was ever **CREATED**!

Even though they are of **One** heart, **One** mind, **One** spirit, and **One** purpose, they are not the same entity. Again, just as a Husband and Wife, are said to be One! Yet, they are not the same person!

Once again: Remember what it said in the Book of John chapter seventeen?

John 17:22-24 (NASB)

²² "And the glory which Thou hast given Me I have given to them; that they may be **One**, just as We are **One**;
²³ I in them, and Thou in Me, that they may be perfected in unity, that the world may know that Thou didst love Me."
²⁴ "Father, I desire that they also, whom Thou hast given Me, be with Me where I am, in order that they may behold My glory, which Thou hast given Me;

for Thou didst love Me

Before The Foundation of The World.

Again: If being One with Almighty God, makes Jesus God. Then for us to be One with Jesus, then this would also make us One with Almighty God, as well. Wouldn't that mean, that we are also **Gods**? **If it made Jesus God?** Are we then to **worship one another** ? ? ? ? ? ? ? ? ?

Jesus is the **Son of God**!

Jesus is **not** - His own **Father**!

Jesus is **not** - יהוה Yehovah (*Jehovah*)!

Jesus is **not** - God Almighty!

Co-Equal ???????

Here we see that **The Ancient of Days**, who is the Heavenly Father, Almighty God that is Supreme, Unparalleled, and Sovereign, over all of Creation. Takes His Seat on His Throne as He Reigns over all The Universe. With **none** to Equal Him*!* Even though most Christians believe The Heavenly Father and JESUS, along with The Holy Spirit are all Co-Equal.

Daniel 7:9-10 (NASB)

The Ancient of Days Reigns

⁹ "I kept looking until thrones were set up,
(*perhaps, before the Twenty-Four Elders*)
And the Ancient of Days took *His* seat; (*on His own Throne*)
His garment *was* white as snow,
And the hair of His head like pure wool.
His throne *was* ablaze with flames,
Its wheels *were* a burning fire.
¹⁰ A river of fire was flowing
And coming out from before Him;
Thousands upon thousands were serving Him,
And myriads upon myriads were standing before Him;
The court convened,
And the books were opened.

Notice, in the following verses of Daniel, that there is no reason for **The Ancient of Days** to be giving **The Son of Man** anything if they were truly **Co-Equal**. **He would already have it***!* But we see that **The Son of Man** does **not** yet have it. Until **The Ancient of Days gives it to Him***!*

Daniel 7:13-14 (NASB)

The Son of Man Presented

(*Words in parentheses - were added for clarity*)
¹³ "I kept looking in the night visions,
And behold, with the clouds of heaven
One like the **Son of Man** was coming,
And He came up to **The Ancient of Days**
And was presented before Him (*the Ancient of Days*).
¹⁴ "And to Him (*the Son of Man*) **was given**
(*by the Ancient of Days*) Dominion, Glory, and a Kingdom,
That **all the peoples, nations, and men of every language**
Might serve Him.
His dominion is an everlasting dominion
Which will not pass away;
And His Kingdom is one
Which will not be destroyed.

> The **Son of Man** does not receive His Kingdom until **Almighty God**, who is **The Ancient of Days** presents it to Him (*The Son of Man*).

Chapter 5 — Co-Equal ?

We see that the Soveran King of the Universe, **The Ancient of Days**, will at that time establish **The Son of Man** as His Sub-ordinate King, over Planet Earth*!* We see this being re-affirmed, in Psalm one hundred and ten.

Psalm 110 (LITV)
(Jay P. Green's - Literal Translation)

The Lord Gives Dominion to the King.

¹ A statement of **Jehovah** to my Lord: Sit at My right hand, until I place your enemies as your footstool.
² **Jehovah** shall send the rod of Your strength out of Zion; rule in the midst of Your enemies.
³ Your people *shall be* willing in the day of Your power; in the majesties of holiness from the womb of the dawn, to You *is* the dew of Your youth.
⁴ **Jehovah** has sworn and will not repent: You are a priest forever according to the order of Melchizedek.
⁵ The Lord at Your (*Jehovah's*) right hand shatters kings in the day of His anger.
⁶ He shall judge among the nations; He shall fill with dead bodies; He shall shatter chiefs over much land.
⁷ He shall drink out of the brook on the way; therefore, He shall lift up the head.

Psalm 2 (LITV)
(Jay P. Green's - Literal Translation)
(*Words in parentheses - were added for clarity*)

The Reign of the Lord's Anointed.

¹ Why have the nations raged,
 and the people are meditating on vanity?
² The kings of the earth set themselves; yea,
 the rulers have plotted together against
Jehovah (יְהֹוָה - *Yehovah*) and **His Anointed** (*Messiah*), saying,
³ We will break their bands (*of restraint*) in two,
 and throw off their cords (*of control*) from us.
⁴ He who sits in the heavens shall laugh;
Jehovah (יְהֹוָה - *Yehovah*) shall mock at them.
⁵ Then He will speak to them in His anger,
 and He will terrify them in His wrath;
⁶ Yea, I have set My king on My holy mount, on Zion.
⁷ (*The King*) I will declare concerning the statute of **Jehovah** (*Yehovah*):
He said to Me, **You are My Son**. Today I have begotten You.
⁸ Ask of Me, and <u>**I will give**</u> the nations as Your inheritance;
and the uttermost parts of the earth as Your possession.
⁹ You shall break them with a rod of iron;
You shall dash them in pieces like a potter's vessel.
¹⁰ Now, then, be wise, O kings; be taught, O judges of the earth:
¹¹ Serve **Jehovah** (יְהֹוָה - *Yehovah*) with fear; yea, rejoice with trembling.

¹² Kiss **The Son** (*pay proper homage to Him*), lest He be angry, and you perish from the way, when His wrath is kindled but a little. O, the blessings of all those who are fleeing to Him for refuge!

We see that it is Jehovah (יְהֹוָה - *Yehovah*) who is **The Ancient of Days,** that has the ultimate supreme power in the Universe. He says to His Son, <u>I will give</u> the nations as Your inheritance, as well as the uttermost parts of the earth as Your possession. This once again shows that The Father and The Son are **not** Co-Equal*!*

John 16:23-24 (NKJV)

²³ "And in that day (*after the Resurrection*) you will ask Me nothing. Most assuredly, I say to you, whatever you ask the Father in My name He will give you. ²⁴ Until now you have asked nothing in My name. Ask, and you will receive, that your joy may be full.

Re-affirming, that even after His Death, Burial, and Resurrection, it is His Father that is far greater, than Himself - JESUS*!*

The origin of the Gentile-Churches Perspective on the Trinity.

Around the mid to late second century, Gentile-Christianity started having varying stand points with one another about different doctrinal positions. Which was different from most of the Jewish-Christians.

The Gentile form of Christianity was seen by Constantine, as one of the means of maintaining control in the Roman Empire. Just as paganism had been used previously for that same purpose in the Empire. So, Constantine sought to unite the various rituals of these different forms of Gentile-Christianity.

The **First Council of Nicaea** was a council of Gentile-Christian bishops convened in the Bithynian city of Nicaea by the Roman Emperor Constantine I in AD 325.

This ecumenical council was the first effort to attain consensus in the Gentile-Church through an assembly representing most of Gentile-Christendom.

The main accomplishments of this Council were: The settlement of the Christological issue in the Gentile-Church, of the divine nature of God the Son and his relationship to God the Father. The construction of the first part of the Nicene Creed. Establishing the uniform observance of the date of Easter. As well as, the promulgation of early Canon Law. (*The early Gentile-Church-Fathers were now doing the same thing as the Scribes and Pharisees had done. They were both adding to, and taking away from, The Laws of God, in order to produce their Canon Law*)

> (*Taken from - The Letter of the Council of Nicaea to the Alexandrians*)
> *We also send you the good news of the settlement concerning the holy feast of Pasch (Passover), namely that in answer to your prayers this question also has been resolved. All the brethren in the East who have hitherto followed the **Jewish practice** will henceforth observe the custom of the Romans and of yourselves and of all of us who from ancient times have kept Easter together with you.*

Historically significant as the first effort to attain consensus in the church through an assembly representing most of Gentile-Christendom was. The Council was the first occasion where the technical aspects of Gentile-Christology were discussed. Through it a precedent was set for subsequent general councils to adopt creeds and canons (*thereby, as stated before, doing the same thing as the Scribes and Pharisees*). This council is generally considered the beginning of the period of the First seven Ecumenical Councils in the History of Gentile-Christianity.

The First Council of Nicaea in 325, set forth the basic concept of the Trinity and was tweaked or refined a little more in the First Council of Constantinople in 381. This established what was to become, the basic view of the Trinity, for nearly all of the Gentile-Church. And affected how St. Jerome believed concerning the Trinity.

St. Jerome was born in Stridon in 347 (*after the Council of Nicaea in 325*). He went to Rome as a student where he learned Latin and studied Christian Theology. He later made a revision of the Latin Bible, based on the Greek manuscripts of the New Testament and the Septuagint, translating much of what became the Latin Vulgate. Jerome died in 420 near Bethlehem.

Around 378 he visited the Nazarenes (Jewish-Christians) of **Berea** (or **Beroea**) which was an ancient city in Macedonia, Northern Greece. In order to examine their copy of a Hebrew gospel, which was said to be the original Gospel of Matthew.

During the late fourth and early fifth centuries Jerome had decided to spend the later part of his life in and around the Holy Land. During this time, he continued to come in contact with many of the Judaeo-Christians (*Nazarenes*) of the region. Jerome noted that the religion practiced by these Nazarenes or Jewish-Christians was dramatically different from the Gentile-Christianity which he and the rest of those in the Roman Empire practiced*!*

Probably one of the most concise and short assessments of this difference was made in a single short comment, about the Judaeo-Christians. Referring to Judaeo-Christians, Jerome said:

"Being both Jewish and Christian, they are neither Jewish nor Christian!"

The basic difference in the Judaeo-Christian Theology and Gentile-Christian Theology can be seen in the New Testament. In the BOOK OF ACTS, we see how the Jewish-Christians viewed the Commandments and Laws of God.

Acts 21:20 (NASB)
[20] ... "You see, brother, how many thousands there are among the Jews of those who have believed, and they are all <u>zealous</u> for **THE LAW**; ..."

We see that Paul was already having trouble with the Gentiles wanting to make their Christianity a separate and distinct religion. In Romans 11:11-24, Paul in his own way is telling the Romans not to break off and become a New and Separate Religion, apart from Judaism, their root. Which sadly is exactly what happened. Just as the Scribes and Pharisees had done, the Gentile-Church Fathers were now doing the same. Both adding to and taking away from The Laws of God!

This difference would be most evident with the foundational concept of the Trinity. Where the Judaeo-Christians believed that JESUS and the Holy Spirit were sub-ordinate to Almighty God, the One and Only True God. With JESUS returning and being established as King over the Earth. Over all the peoples, nations, and men of every language on this Planet.

However, as we touched on earlier, Constantine saw Gentile-Christianity as one of the methods of maintaining control in the Roman Empire. Just as paganism had been used previously in the Empire for that same purpose. At the First Council of Nicaea (325) also brought into more prominence the Gentile view of the Trinity. We see that because of the multiple Pagan Gods were considered the norm. The Father, Son and Holy Spirit, were supposed to be three manifestations of the One God. In order to not violate the first of The Ten Commandments.

Whereas the Jewish-Christians believed that there was only One God, with JESUS and the Holy Spirit being sub-ordinate to Almighty God, in the Trinity. With JESUS being The Firstborn Creation of the Heavenly Father! (*As we saw in the last Chapter.*)

Colossians 1:15 (NIV)
¹⁵ The Son is the image of the invisible God, the <u>**firstborn**</u> over <u>**All Creation**</u>.

Proverbs 8:22-31 (NIV)
²² "The LORD <u>brought me forth</u> as <u>the first of His works</u>, **<u>before</u> His deeds of old**;
²³ I was appointed from eternity, from the beginning, **<u>before</u> the world began**. When there were no oceans, **I was given birth**,
²⁴ when there were no springs abounding with water;
²⁵ <u>before</u> the mountains were settled in place, <u>before</u> the hills, **I was given birth**,
²⁶ <u>before</u> He made the earth or its fields or any of the dust of the world.
²⁷ <u>I was there</u> when He set the heavens in place, when He marked out the horizon on the face of the deep,
²⁸ when He established the clouds above and fixed securely the fountains of the deep,
²⁹ when He gave the sea its boundary so the waters would not overstep His command, and when He marked out the foundations of the earth.
³⁰ Then <u>I was the craftsman</u> **at His side**. I was filled with delight day after day, rejoicing always in His presence,
³¹ rejoicing in His whole world and delighting in mankind."

The Book of Proverbs is a collection of unrelated proverbs, assembled into a single book. To show where one proverb stops and the next begins, the Hebrew codex used for translating most of the English versions of the Bible, has the Hebrew letter פ placed at the end of a proverbial section to indicate where one stops and the other starts. Proverb chapter eight has a פ at the end of verse 21 (just before the beginning of verse 22) and at the end of verse 31. Showing that it is un-connected and un-related to the proverbs both before it and after it*!*

As mentioned earlier, the Gentile-Church was faced with having to deal with The First Commandment; they eventually developed the belief that The Almighty God, JESUS, and The Holy Spirit were Co-Equal and different manifestations of Only One God.

For many years after the Crucifixion of JESUS, those who had been taught by JESUS, in person, for years during JESUS's ministry, were still keeping The LAWS OF GOD that applied to them! Also, *don't forget*, that the New Testament shows that JESUS had appeared to many, if not most, of these people after His resurrection; teaching and instructing them on how to proceed.

Yet today most, if not all, of Gentile-Christianity claims that JESUS did away with THE LAW and instituted **"Grace"** as the only means for the True Believer to become saved and receive ETERNAL LIFE! Yet, most of them do not realize what the Biblical meaning of **Grace** actually is.

> The Biblical Definition For - The **"Grace"** of God
> (*5485*) - The divine influence upon the heart;
> and its reflection in the life (*of the individual*).
> Resulting in receiving unmerited favor from God.

(*from Strong's Concordance*)

> **"Grace"** does **not** mean **"forgiveness"**!
> It is **not** a **"get out of Hell"** free card!

However, *as was pointed out earlier*, many if not most of these Jewish believers in Jerusalem, mentioned in the BOOK OF ACTS, had the privilege of being taught by THE MESSIAH, face to face, during His earthly ministry. As well as having had the advantage, and the blessing, of having JESUS appear to them after his resurrection, to explain what all of this meant and how to proceed. These Believers in the BOOK OF ACTS, never refrained from offering Animal Sacrifices while there was still a Temple. Nor did they stop adhering to any of The LAWS OF GOD! At least to the very best of their God given ability.

They did not believe that the Trinity was three manifestations of One God. They believed that Almighty God was supreme with JESUS and The Holy Spirit being part of Creation and therefore, sub-ordinate to The Almighty. With **The Ancient of Days** giving planet Earth to His Son, as His possession in the future.

The question is: "Were these Judaeo-Christians *wrong* to follow JESUS and worship in the manner that He, JESUS, taught them to worship?

Or, N<u>OT</u>?

The Word was GOD?

This is what most people have been taught about Jesus. Because He was the Word and the Word was made flesh and dwelled among us, as a human here on this earth.

But is this right? Are the Churches accurate in their understanding of Jesus being GOD?

You do have to admit; that at first glance, when you are reading the book of John, in most of the various English translations, that does appear to be the case.

However, on closer examination of both the Greek text of the New Testament and the Hebrew text of the Old Testament, along with a basic understanding of some of the unique and distinctive aspects of each language; it then becomes obvious, that it is **not** so cut and dry, as it first appears to be, in most of the English translations.

So, let's take a look at each of these scriptures and the various linguistic aspects that are associated with each one of them. Starting with John 1:1, or better yet, let's make it John 1:1-3.

John 1:1-3 (NIV)
¹ In The beginning was the Word, and the Word was with GOD, and the Word was GOD.
² He was with GOD in the beginning.
³ Through him all things were made; without him nothing was made that has been made.

We will start by looking at just the first verse of John one.

John 1:1 (NIV)
¹ In The beginning was the Word, and the Word was with GOD, and the Word was GOD.

In English, this appears to most Christians as though it is saying that Jesus is GOD. But before we go on much further, we need to look at the source from which the English was derived. It will be of great importance in setting the stage, for a more accurate understanding of this passage of Scripture. To do this, we will take a look at the original Greek text. The text from which the English translators derived, "… and the Word was GOD".

In J.P. Green's Interlinear of the Bible, we can see that it shows the Strong's numbers above and the English below, with the Greek in between.

1722	746	2258	3056		3056	2258	4314		2316	2316 2258	3056
Ἐν	ἀρχῇ	ἦν	ὁ λόγος,	καί	ὁ λόγος	ἦν	πρός	τόν	θεόν,	καί θεός ἦν	ὁ λόγος.
In (the)	beginning	was	the Word,	and	the Word		was	with	- God,	and God was	the Word.

John 1:1

To Love GOD!

In the Greek language, the Greek word θεόν (*god*) or θεὸς (*god*) can be referring to any one of a number of Greek gods in their Pantheon of gods. Or even to any of the other gods in the Near East and/or the Mediterranean region. Which included THEE GOD OF ABRAHAM, ISAAC AND JACOB. The manner in which the authors of the Greek New Testament made the distinction between the GOD of the Bible and the Pagan gods, was to <u>always</u> place one of the Greek **definite articles** in front of the Greek word for god. Declaring "THEE GOD"! Which was also done in the Septuagint. In John 1:1 there are two definite articles used in the sentence. The article ὁ is used three times before the Greek word for "Word" λόγος. The article τόν is used once before the Greek word θεόν (GOD). Yet the word θεὸς (*god*) does **not** have any article before it. **Why?**

*(the following is taken **mostly** from J.P. Green's Interlinear)*

1722	746	2258	3056		3056	2258	4314	2316		2316	2258	3056
Ἐν	ἀρχῇ	ἦν	ὁ λόγος,	καὶ	ὁ λόγος	ἦν	πρός	τόν θεόν,	καὶ	θεὸς	ἦν	ὁ λόγος.
In (the)	beginning	was	<u>the</u> Word,	and	<u>the</u> Word	was	with	**thee** God,	and	God	was	<u>the</u> Word

John 1:1

So, why is there no article in front of θεὸς (*god*) and what is this telling those people who know and understand the original New Testament Greek? As well as the Greek of the Septuagint.

If you look in **THE EXPOSITOR'S GREEK TESTAMENT** edited by The Rev. W. Robertson Nicoll, M.A., LL.D. (Editor of "The Expositor," "The expositor's Bible," Etc.) **VOLUME I. Part II, THE GOSPEL OF ST. JOHN**, By The Rev. Marcus Dods, D.D. Professor of Exegetical Theology, New Collage, Edinburgh; published by WM. B. Eerdmans Publishing Company Grand Rapids, Michigan U.S.A. - On page 684 we find the following:

> (3) **The Word** is distinguishable from GOD and yet θεὸς ἦν ὁ λόγος, **the Word** was GOD of Divine nature; <u>**not**</u> "a GOD," which to a Jewish ear would have been abominable; nor yet identical with all that can be called GOD, for then the article would have been inserted.

If you also look in, The New **LINGUISTIC** and **EXEGETICAL** Key To The **GREEK NEW TESTAMENT**, By Cleon L. Rogers Jr. & Cleon L. Rogers III, published by Zondervan Publishing House Grand Rapids, Michigan; when you check in The section entitled: **The Gospel of John**, on page 175 you will find the following:

> θεὸς (#2536) GOD. The word (θεὸς) occurs without the art. (article). It is the predicate emphasizing quality "the **Word** has the same nature as GOD".

Both of these sources (*as well as others*) show that because there is no definite article in front of the word θεὸς (*god*) that it is saying, the Word or <u>Jesus</u> (*Yeshua*) <u>was the reflection of the nature and character of GOD</u>. **However**, even though a reflection is the image of what is being reflected, it does not have the same substance as **Thee One** who is being reflected. Perhaps this is why Jesus said; "… **Anyone who has seen me has seen the Father.** …" in John 14:9. But just a few verses later, Jesus also said; "… **the Father is GREATER than I**." in John 14:28. Thereby declaring that they are **not** the same Entity or Person! And that He (*Jesus or Yeshua*) is <u>**sub-ordinate**</u> to His Heavenly Father!

2ed Corinthians 4:4 (NIV)

⁴ The god of this age has blinded the minds of unbelievers, so that they cannot see the light of the gospel of the glory of Christ, <u>who is the image of God</u>.

Colossians 1:15 (NASB)

¹⁵ And He is the **image** of the invisible God, the **first-born** of all creation.

So, once again, just to review and hopefully better grasp what Jesus is declaring. Being the *reflection* and *image* of God is why Jesus could **truthfully,** say in both of the following quotes:

John 14:9 (NIV)

⁹ Jesus answered: "Don't you know me, Philip, even after I have been among you such a long time? Anyone who has seen Me has seen the Father. How can you say, "Show us the Father?

And, just a few verses later He said,

John 14:28 (NIV)

²⁸ "You heard me say, 'I am going away and I am coming back to you.' If you love me, you would be glad that I am going to the Father, for **the Father is GREATER than I**."

This would also explain why Jesus (*Yeshua*) also told everyone <u>**not**</u> to pray to Him**!**

John 16:23 (NKJV)

²³ "And in that day, you will <u>ask Me</u> **nothing**. Most assuredly, I say to you, whatever you ask the **Father** in My name He will give you."

Whatever is being reflected is greater than its reflection! Even though Jesus is the reflection of God, Jesus is <u>**not**</u> His Own Father!

John 20:17 (NKJV)

¹⁷ Jesus said to her, "Do not cling to Me, for I have not yet ascended to My Father; but go to My brethren and say to them, 'I am ascending to **My Father** and **your Father**, and *to* **My God** and **your God**.'"

Notice: After the Resurrection, who Jesus said, is to be **your God***!*

We are <u>**not**</u> to pray to the reflection of God, but rather to God Himself! We are to do so, in the name and power given to us by the individual, who is God's reflection!

Yet, in many translations the translators, shall we say, tend to fudge when it comes to adding in their own personal theology, to the text of what they are translating.

John 1:18

KJV	NASB	NIV
¹⁸ No man hath seen GOD at any time; the only begotten Son, which is in the bosom of the Father, he hath declared *him*.	¹⁸ No man has seen GOD at any time; the only begotten GOD, who is in the bosom of the Father, He has explained *Him*.	¹⁸ No one has ever seen GOD, but GOD the One and Only, who is at the Father's side, has made him known.

John 1:18

```
2316    3762    3708    4415        3439            5207
Θεον   ουδεις  εωρακε  πωποτε   ὁ  μονογενης      υἱός
God    No one has seen at any time; the only-begotten Son,

5607/1519   3859        3962    1565      1834
ὁ ὢν εἰς τὸν κόλπον τοῦ πατρός, ἐκεῖνος ἐξηγήσατο.
who is in the bosom of the Father, that One explains (Him)
```

(from J.P. Green's Interlinear)

Notice that the New American Standard takes the liberty to change the translation of the Greek word for **"Son"** to **"GOD"**. The New International Version also "**falsely**" claims that the **"Son is the One and Only GOD"** who is at the side of the **Father**. When it is the **Father**, that is "**The One and Only GOD.**" With **His Son**, sitting at **His** side*!* (*Which is in the bosom of the Father.*)

Psalm 2 (LITV)

(Jay P. Green's - Literal Translation)

(Words in parentheses - were added for clarity)

¹ Why have the nations raged, and the people are meditating on vanity?

² The kings of the earth set themselves; yea, the rulers have plotted together against Jehovah (יְהֹוָה - YEHOVAH) and His Anointed (*Messiah*), saying,

³ We will break their bands (*of restraint*) in two, and throw off their cords (*of control*) from us.

⁴ He who sits in the heavens shall laugh; Jehovah (יְהֹוָה - YEHOVAH) shall mock at them.

⁵ Then He will speak to them in His anger, and He will terrify them in His wrath;

⁶ Yea, I have set My king on My holy mount, on Zion.

⁷ (*The King*) I will declare concerning the statute of Jehovah (*YEHOVAH*): He said to Me, You are My Son. Today I have begotten You.

⁸ Ask of Me, and **I will give** the nations as Your inheritance; and the uttermost parts of the earth as Your possession.
⁹ You shall break them with a rod of iron; You shall dash them in pieces like a potter's vessel.
¹⁰ Now, then, be wise, O kings; be taught, O judges of the earth:
¹¹ Serve Jehovah (יְהֹוָה - YEHOVAH) with fear; yea, rejoice with trembling.
¹² Kiss the Son (*pay proper homage to Him*), lest He be angry, and you perish from the way, when His wrath is kindled but a little. Oh, the blessings of all those who are fleeing to Him for refuge!

After Yehovah **gives** the nations to His Son as well as the uttermost parts of the earth as His possession. We see that in verse twelve, that Almighty GOD, The Heavenly Father, יְהֹוָה **YEHOVAH** (*Jehovah*) expects everyone to give proper honor and respect to **His Son**! Even though, יְהֹוָה **YEHOVAH** (*Jehovah*), still requires us to **only** worship Him; and **NO** other!

We are to have **NO** other gods or god!

It does **not** matter whether they are a **real** or **imagined deity**!

He, **alone**, is to be the **only** GOD we worship; and **NO** other!

In verse eight of Psalm two, The Heavenly Father, Almighty GOD, יְהֹוָה **YEHOVAH** (*Jehovah*) is telling **His Son**, Jesus (*Yeshua*); "Ask of Me, and **I will give** the nations as Your inheritance; and the uttermost parts of the earth as Your possession."

Daniel is given a vision, of when this transpires!

Daniel 7:13-14 (NASB)

(*Words in parentheses - were added for clarity*)
¹³ "I kept looking in the night visions,
And behold, with the clouds of heaven
One like the **Son of Man** was coming,
And He came up to **The Ancient of Days**
And was presented before Him (*the Ancient of Days*).
¹⁴ "And to Him (*the Son of Man*) **was given**
(*by the Ancient of Days*) Dominion, Glory and a Kingdom,
That **all the peoples, nations, and men of every language**
Might serve Him.
His dominion is an everlasting dominion
Which will not pass away;
And His Kingdom is one
Which will not be destroyed.

IT IS **THE ANCIENT OF DAYS, ALMIGHTY GOD, THE KING OF THE UNIVERSE, WHO RULES OVER ALL THE RIGHTEOUS ANGELIC HOST** throughout **ALL OF THIS UNIVERSE, FROM ONE END OF THE HEAVENS TO THE OTHER**. Who will at that time install **THE SON OF MAN** as His sub-ordinate **KING**, over all of the inhabitants of **Planet Earth!** Which is a single, small, mostly blue planet, with white clouds, circling an insignificant sun, near the edge of the Milky Way Galaxy. Which is only one of millions of millions of Galaxies in the Universe which **Almighty GOD** rules over.

Our Milky Way Galaxy is itself, made up of millions of different solar systems, of which our sun and its solar system is just one. When **THE SON OF MAN** is to be installed by **THE ANCIENT OF DAYS** as **His** sub-ordinate **KING**, over the inhabitants of this single, solitary planet, upon which we live. He will be placed over all the people of every nation and the men of every language, who are upon this single, small, mostly blue, planet with white clouds, which we know as **Earth!**

Jesus (*Yeshua*) has only One **GOD**, **YEHOVAH** (*Jehovah*) who is **THE ANCIENT OF DAYS**; which **He Worships and Loves**, with **All** of **His Heart**, **All** of **His Soul** and **All** of **His Might** *!*

Notice: that the Dominion, Glory and Kingdom is **not** His for the taking*!* But rather it is given to Him, by **GOD**, **HIS HEAVENLY FATHER***!*

Daniel 7:14 (NASB)

(Words in parentheses - were added for clarity)

¹⁴ "And to Him (*the Son of Man*) **was given**
(*by the Ancient of Days*) Dominion, Glory and a Kingdom,
That **all the peoples, nations, and men of every language**
Might serve Him. …"

Psalm 2:8 (LITV)

(Jay P. Green's - Literal Translation)

⁸ Ask of Me, and **I will give** the nations as Your inheritance;
and the uttermost parts of the earth as Your possession.

Matthew 28:18 (NASB)

¹⁸ And Jesus came up and spoke to them, saying,
"**All authority** in heaven and on earth **has been given** to Me."

Remember: He did **not** have "**All Authority**" until after **YEHOVAH** (יְהֹוָה - *Jehovah*) **His Heavenly Father** - gave it - to Him*!* Just as Joseph did **not** have all of the power and authority in Egypt until Pharaoh - gave it - to him*!* Even so, obviously, that did **not** make Joseph, Pharaoh*!*

Just as a **King** will sometimes give his son, who is faithfully serving him, or even one of his faithful servants, the **power and authority** to act in **the name of the King**. That alone does **not** make him **King**. Even though he is acting in the **name, power and authority** of the **King**.

We see that **Jesus** (*Yeshua*) is acting in the **Name, Power and Authority** of **His Heavenly Father** (יְהֹוָה - *YEHOVAH - Jehovah*), which He is using on His Father's behalf. However, even though

Jesus (*Yeshua*) has been **given** "**All Power and Authority**", that does **not** make **Jesus** (*Yeshua*) his own **Father**! It does **not** make him **GOD Almighty**! Even though he is acting with that same **Name, Power and Authority**! Because "**All Authority**" has been **given** to him, to **use**!

John 5:19-27 (NASB)

¹⁹ Therefore Jesus answered and was saying to them, "Truly, truly, I say to you, the Son can do nothing of Himself, unless *it is* something He sees the Father doing; for whatever the Father does, these things the Son also does in the same way.
²⁰ For the Father loves the Son and shows Him all things that He Himself is doing; and *the Father* will show Him greater works than these, so that you will be amazed.
²¹ For just as the Father raises the dead and **gives** them life, so the Son **also gives** life to whom He wishes.
²² For not even the Father judges anyone, but **He has given** all judgment to the Son,
²³ so that all will honor the Son (*honor **not** Worship*) just as they honor the Father. The one who does not honor the Son does not honor the Father **who sent Him**.
²⁴ "Truly, truly, I say to you, the one who hears My word, and believes Him **who sent Me**, has **Eternal Life**, and does not come into judgment, but has passed out of death into life.
²⁵ Truly, truly, I say to you, a time is coming and even now has arrived, when the dead will hear the voice of the Son of GOD, and those who hear will live.
²⁶ For just as the Father has life in Himself, so **He gave** to the Son also to have life in Himself;
²⁷ and **He gave** Him authority to execute judgment, because He is *the* Son of Man.

John 6:38 (NASB)

³⁸ For I have come down from heaven, **not** to do My own will, but the **will of Him who sent Me**.

Matthew 11:27 (NASB)

²⁷ **All things have been handed over to Me** by My Father; and no one knows the Son except the Father; nor does anyone know the Father except the Son, and anyone to whom the Son determines to reveal *Him*.

John 5:30 (NASB)

³⁰ "**I can do nothing on My own initiative**. As I hear, I judge; and My judgment is just, because **I do not seek My own will, but the will of Him who sent Me**.

John 3:35-36 (NASB)

³⁵ The Father loves the Son and **has entrusted all things** to His hand.

³⁶ The one who believes in the Son (*believes **not** Worships*) has **Eternal Life**; but the one who does not obey the Son will not see life, but the wrath of GOD remains on him."

John 7:28-29 (NASB)

²⁸ Then Jesus cried out in the temple, teaching and saying, "You both know Me and know where I am from; and I have **not** come of Myself, but **He who sent Me is true**, whom you do not know. ²⁹ I know Him, because I am from Him, and **He sent Me**."

Matthew 26:64 (NASB)

⁶⁴ Jesus said to him, "You have said *it* yourself. But I tell you, from now *on* you will see the Son of Man **sitting at the right hand of power,** and coming on the clouds of heaven."

John 8:28 (NASB)

²⁸ So Jesus said, "When you lift up the **Son of Man**, then you will know that I am *He*, and **I do nothing on My own initiative**, but **I speak these things as the Father taught Me.**

John 17:1-5 (NASB)

¹ Jesus spoke these things; and raising His eyes to heaven, He said, "Father, the hour has come; glorify Your Son, so that the Son may glorify You,

² just as **You gave** Him authority over all mankind, so that to all whom **You have given** Him, He may give **Eternal Life**.

³ And this is **Eternal Life**,

> that they may know You,
> **The Only True GOD**,
> and Jesus Christ whom
> **You have sent**.

⁴ I glorified You on the earth by accomplishing the work which **You have given** Me to do.
⁵ And now You, Father, glorify Me together with You before the world existed.
⁶ "I have revealed Your name to the men whom **You gave** Me out of the world; they were Yours and **You gave** them to Me, and they have followed Your word."
⁷ "Now they have come to know that everything which **You have given Me** is from **You**;

⁸ for the words which **You gave Me** I have given to them; and they received *them* and truly understood that **I came forth from You**, and they believed that **You sent Me**."

Colossians 1:15 (NASB)
¹⁵ And He is the **image** of the invisible GOD, the **first-born** of all creation.

Proverbs 8:22-31 (NIV)
²² "The LORD brought me forth as the first of His works, before His deeds of old;
²³ I was appointed from eternity, from the beginning, **before the world began**.
²⁴ When there were no oceans, **I was given birth**, when there were no springs abounding with water;
²⁵ before the mountains were settled in place, before the hills, **I was given birth**,
²⁶ before He made the earth or its fields or any of the dust of the world.
²⁷ I was there when He set the heavens in place, when He marked out the horizon on the face of the deep,
²⁸ when He established the clouds above and fixed securely the fountains of the deep,
²⁹ when He gave the sea its boundary so the waters would not overstep His command, and when He marked out the foundations of the earth.
³⁰ Then I was the craftsman **at His side**.

> **John 1:2-3** (NIV)
> ² He was with GOD in the beginning.
> ³ Through him all things were made; without him **nothing** was made that has been made.

I was filled with delight day after day, rejoicing always in His presence,
³¹ rejoicing in His whole world and delighting in mankind."

> The Book of Proverbs is a collection of unrelated proverbs, assembled into a single book. To show where one proverb stops and the next begins, the Hebrew codex used for translating most of the English versions of the Bible, has the Hebrew letter פ placed at the end of a proverbial section to indicate where one stops and the other starts. Proverbs chapter eight has a פ at the end of verse 21 (*just before the beginning of verse 22*) and at the end of verse 31. Showing that it is un-connected and un-related to the proverbs both before it and after it*!*

Luke 10:21-22 (NASB)

²¹ At that very time He rejoiced greatly in the Holy Spirit, and said, "I praise You, Father, Lord of heaven and earth, that You have hidden these things from *the* wise and intelligent and have revealed them to infants. Yes, Father, for *doing* so was well-pleasing in Your sight.
²² **All things have been handed over to Me** by My Father, and no one knows who the Son is except the Father, and who the Father is except the Son, and anyone to whom the Son determines to reveal *Him*."

John 8:42 (NASB)

⁴² Jesus said to them, "If GOD were your Father, you would love Me, for I proceeded forth and have come from GOD, **for I have not even come on My own initiative**, but **He sent Me**.

John 5:44 (NASB)

⁴⁴ How can you believe, when you accept glory from one another and you do not seek the glory that is from **The *One and* Only GOD?**

John 12:49 (NASB)

⁴⁹ For I did **not** speak **on My own initiative**, but the Father Himself **who sent Me** has **given Me** a commandment *as to* what to say and what to speak.

Ephesians 1:15-23 (NASB)

(Words in parentheses - were added for clarity)

¹⁵ For this reason I too, having heard of the faith in the Lord Jesus which *exists* among you and your love for all the saints,
¹⁶ do not cease giving thanks for you, while making mention *of you* in my prayers;
¹⁷ that **The GOD** of our Lord Jesus Christ, **The Father of Glory**, may give you a spirit of wisdom and of revelation in the knowledge of Him. *(Jesus)*
¹⁸ *I pray that* the eyes of your heart may be enlightened, so that you will know what is the hope of His *(Jesus's)* calling, what are the riches of the glory of His *(Jesus's)* inheritance in the saints,
¹⁹ and what is the boundless greatness of His *(GOD, Jesus or both?)* power toward us who believe. *These are* in accordance with the working of the strength of His *(GOD's)* might
²⁰ which He *(GOD)* brought about in Christ, when He *(GOD)* raised Him *(Jesus)* from the dead and seated Him *(Jesus)* at His *(GOD, The Father's)* right hand in the heavenly *places,*
²¹ far above all rule and authority and power and dominion, and every name that is named, not only in this age but also in the one to come.

²² And He (GOD) put all things in subjection under His (Jesus's) feet, and made Him (Jesus) head over all things to the church,
²³ which is His (Jesus's) body, the fullness of Him who fills all in all.

Philippians 2:5-10 (NKJV)

⁵ Let this mind be in you, which was also in Christ Jesus,
⁶ who, being in the form (*image and likeness*) of GOD, did not consider it robbery to be (ἴσος - *similar to, or like*) equal with GOD,

> *2470.* **ἴσος** *isŏs, ee'-sos*: prob. from *1492* (through the idea of seeming); *similar* (in amount or kind):- + agree, as much, equal, like.
> (*from Strong's Concordance*)

⁷ but made Himself of no reputation, taking the form of a bondservant, *and* coming in the likeness of men.
⁸ And being found in appearance as a man, He humbled Himself and became obedient to *the point of* death, even the death of the cross.
⁹ Therefore **GOD also has highly exalted Him** and **given Him** the name, which is above every name,
¹⁰ that at the name of Jesus every knee should bow, of those in heaven, and of those on earth, and of those under the earth,

Mark 16:15-19 (NASB)

¹⁵ And He said to them, "Go into all the world and preach the gospel to all creation.
¹⁶ The one who **has** believed (*believed **not** Worshiped*) and has been baptized will be saved; but the one who has **not** believed will be condemned.
¹⁷ These signs will accompany those who **have** believed (*believed **not** Worshiped*): in My name they will cast out demons, they will speak with new tongues;
¹⁸ they will pick up serpents, and if they drink any deadly *poison*, it will not harm them; they will lay hands on the sick, and they will recover."
¹⁹ So then, when the Lord Jesus had spoken to them, He was received up into heaven and sat down at the **right hand of GOD.**

Pay close attention, in chapter sixteen of Mark, in verses sixteen and seventeen it said: "believed" **not** worshiped*!*

Psalm 110 (LITV)

¹ A statement of Jehovah (יְהֹוָה - *Yehovah*) to my Lord: "Sit at My right hand, until I place Your enemies as Your footstool."
² Jehovah (יְהֹוָה - *Yehovah*) shall send the rod of Your strength out of Zion; rule in the midst of Your enemies.

³ Your people *shall be* willing in the day of Your power; in the majesties of holiness, from the womb of the dawn, to You *as* the dew of Your youth.

⁴ Jehovah (יְהֹוָה - *Yehovah*) has sworn and will not repent: You *are* a priest forever according to the order of **Melchizedek**.

⁵ The Lord (*Jesus - Yeshua*) at Your (יְהֹוָה - YEHOVAH'S - JEHOVAH'S) right hand, shatters kings in the day of His anger.

⁶ He shall judge among the nations; He shall fill with dead bodies; He shall shatter chiefs over much land.

⁷ He shall drink out of the brook on the way; therefore, He shall lift up the head.

1ˢᵗ Corinthians 12:3 (NASB)

³ Therefore I make known to you that no one speaking by the Spirit of GOD says, "Jesus is accursed"; and no one can say, "**Jesus is Lord**," except by the **Holy Spirit**.

Which definition, for the Greek word **κύριος** that was translated as **"Lord"**; do you think the **Holy Spirit** is using?

> *2962.* κύριος kuriŏs, *koo'-ree-os;* from κυρος kurŏs (supremacy): *supreme* in authority, i.e. (as a noun) *controller:* by implication *Mr.* [*Mister*] **Lord**, **Master**, **Sir** or **King** (*also as a respectful title for*) **GOD, LORD**.
> (*from Strong's Concordance*)

1ˢᵗ Corinthians 8:6 (NASB)

⁶ yet for us there is *only* **ONE GOD**, **The Father**, from whom are all things, and we *exist* for Him; and **One Lord, Jesus Christ**, by whom are all things, and we *exist* through Him.

Ephesians 4:4-6 (NASB)

⁴ *There is* one body and one Spirit, just as you also were called in one hope of your calling;

⁵ one Lord, one faith, one baptism,

⁶ **ONE GOD** and **Father** of all who is over all and through all and in all.

The First Commandment
(*Exodus 20:2-3*)

אָנֹכִי יְהוָה אֱלֹהֶיךָ, אֲשֶׁר הוֹצֵאתִיךָ מֵאֶרֶץ מִצְרַיִם מִבֵּית עֲבָדִים: לֹא-יִהְיֶה לְךָ אֱלֹהִים אֲחֵרִים, עַל-פָּנָי.

I am **YEHOVAH** (*Jehovah*) your **GOD**, who brought you out of the land of Egypt, out of the house of bondage. You shall have **NO** other gods, to My Face.

Deuteronomy 32:39 (NASB)

³⁹ See now that I, I am He,
And there is no god besides Me;
It is I *who* put to death and give life.
I have wounded and *it is* I *who* heal,
and there is no one who can save
anyone from My hand.

Isaiah 45:5-7 (NASB)

⁵ **I am the LORD** (יְהוָֹה - *YEHOVAH*), and **there is no one else**;
There is no GOD except Me.
I will arm you, though you have not known Me,
⁶ So that *people* may know from the rising to the setting
of the sun that **there is no one besides Me**.
I am the LORD (יְהוָֹה - *YEHOVAH*), and **there is no one else**,
⁷ The One forming light and creating darkness,
causing well-being and creating disaster;
I am the LORD (יְהוָֹה - *YEHOVAH*) **who does all these things.**

[*see Addendum* – 1]

1 Timothy 1:17 (NASB)

¹⁷ Now to **The King** (*of the Universe*) eternal, immortal, invisible,
the **only GOD**, *be* honor and glory forever and ever. Amen.

John 17:3 (NASB)

³ And this is **Eternal Life**,

that they may know You,
The Only True GOD,
and Jesus Christ whom
You have sent

When you have developed a **Life-Style**,

where you **truly** know and serve **GOD** and **His Son***!*

You will then have reached a point,

where **you** and your **Life-Style**,

will truly **endure forever***!*

When you are given,

Eternal Life*!*

Doubting Thomas

Most people have heard someone, at one time or another, call someone a Doubting Thomas. Or tell someone not to be a Doubting Thomas.

The term **"Doubting Thomas"** comes from the obvious **dis**-belief of Thomas to the resurrection of Jesus, and requiring proof for him to believe it.

John 20:24-25 (NASB)
²⁴ But Thomas, one of the twelve, who was called Didymus, was not with them when Jesus came.
²⁵ So the other disciples were saying to him, "We have seen the Lord!" But he said to them, "Unless I see in His hands the imprint of the nails, and put my finger into the place of the nails, and put my hand into His side, I will not believe."

Thomas's doubt or dis-belief, was addressed by Jesus, in John 20:27-30. Thomas is told to not remain or continue in his doubt and dis-belief.

John 20:27-30 (NASB)
²⁷ Then He said to Thomas, "Place your finger here, and see My hands; and take your hand and put it into My side; and do not continue in disbelief, but *be* a believer."
²⁸ Thomas answered and said to Him, "My Lord and my GOD!"
²⁹ Jesus said to him, "Because you have seen Me, have you *now* believed? Blessed *are* they who did not see, and *yet* believed."

Most people read this and think that Thomas is saying, that Jesus is his Lord and God. But it should be noted: "Him" No.846 (*from Strong's Concordance*) is also translated more than 25 times as "Himself" in the KJV.

John 20:28 (NASB)
²⁸ Thomas answered and said to Him (*or himself*), "My Lord and my GOD!"

The statement in the first part of verse 28 is a narrative of the author, who wrote the book of John. All that Thomas actually said was; **"My Lord and my GOD!"**

Question: Is Thomas referring to **The Heavenly Father** or to **Jesus**?

Because, if Thomas is expressing **a prayer of astonishment**, to his **Heavenly Father**. Then Thomas would **not** be breaking the First Commandment. But if Thomas was directing this statement toward Jesus. Then he would have been breaking the First Commandment.

To Love GOD!

The First Commandment
(*Exodus 20:2-3*)

> אָנֹכִי **יְהֹוָה** אֱלֹהֶיךָ, אֲשֶׁר הוֹצֵאתִיךָ מֵאֶרֶץ מִצְרַיִם מִבֵּית עֲבָדִים:
> **לֹא**-יִהְיֶה לְךָ אֱלֹהִים אֲחֵרִים, עַל-פָּנָי.
>
> I am **YEHOVAH** (*Jehovah*) your GOD, who brought you out of the land of Egypt, out of the house of bondage. You shall have **NO** other gods, to My Face.

Wouldn't this include **Jesus** (*Yeshua*) יֵשׁוּעַ ?

Regardless as to **His Deity**;

He is not **Yehovah** (*Jehovah*) יְהֹוָה

who is **His Heavenly Father.**

Mark 12:28-30 (NASB)

28 One of the scribes came up and heard them arguing, and recognizing that He had answered them well, asked Him, "What commandment is the foremost of all?"
29 Jesus answered, "The foremost is, 'Hear, Israel! The Lord (*Yehovah* יְהֹוָה) is our GOD, the Lord (*Yehovah* יְהֹוָה) is one;
30 and you shall love the Lord (*Yehovah* יְהֹוָה) your GOD with all your heart, and with all your soul, and with all your mind, and with all your strength.' (*this is a quote from Deuteronomy 6:4-5*)

Deuteronomy 6:4-5

> **4** Hear, O Israel: **Yehovah** (יְהֹוָה) is our GOD; **Yehovah** (יְהֹוָה) is One.
>
> שְׁמַע יִשְׂרָאֵל **יְהֹוָה** אֱלֹהֵינוּ **יְהֹוָה** אֶחָד:
>
> **5** And you shall love **Yehovah** (יְהֹוָה), your GOD, with all your heart, and with all your soul, and with all your might.
>
> וְאָהַבְתָּ אֵת **יְהֹוָה** אֱלֹהֶיךָ בְּכָל-לְבָבְךָ וּבְכָל-נַפְשְׁךָ וּבְכָל-מְאֹדֶךָ:

Matthew 22:36-38 (NASB)

36 "Teacher, which is the greatest commandment in the Law?"
37 And He said to him, "'You shall love the Lord (*Yehovah* יְהֹוָה) your GOD with **All your heart**, and with **All your soul**, and with **All your mind**.' (*read - Addendum Number One*)
38 This is the great and foremost commandment. (*Deut. 6:5*)

Luke 4:8 (NASB)

⁸ Jesus replied to him, "It is written: 'You shall worship the Lord (*Yehovah* יְהֹוָה) your GOD and serve Him ONLY.'"

Matthew 4:7 (NASB)

⁷ Jesus said to him, "On the other hand, it is written: 'You shall not put the Lord (*Yehovah* יְהֹוָה) your GOD to the test.'"

John 20:17 (NASB)

¹⁷ Jesus said to her, "Stop clinging to Me, for I have not yet ascended to the Father; but go to My brothers and say to them, 'I am ascending to My Father and your Father, and My GOD and your GOD.'"

Matthew 4:10 (NASB)

¹⁰ Then Jesus said to him, "Go away, Satan! For it is written: 'You shall worship the Lord (*Yehovah* יְהֹוָה) your GOD, and serve Him ONLY.'"

1st Corinthians 8:6 (NASB)

⁶ yet for us there is *only* ONE GOD, The Father, from whom are all things, and we *exist* for Him; and One Lord, Jesus Christ, by whom are all things, and we *exist* through Him.

Ephesians 4:4-6 (NASB)

⁴ *There is* one body and one Spirit, just as you also were called in one hope of your calling;
⁵ one Lord, one faith, one baptism,
⁶ ONE GOD and Father of all who is over all and through all and in all.

Again, let's look at the First Commandment, as well as the conclusion of the last chapter.

The First Commandment
(*Exodus 20:2-3*)

אָנֹכִי **יְהֹוָה** אֱלֹהֶיךָ, אֲשֶׁר הוֹצֵאתִיךָ מֵאֶרֶץ מִצְרַיִם מִבֵּית עֲבָדִים: **לֹא**־יִהְיֶה לְךָ אֱלֹהִים אֲחֵרִים, עַל־פָּנָי.	I am YEHOVAH (*Jehovah*) your GOD, who brought you out of the land of Egypt, out of the house of bondage. You shall have NO other gods, to My Face.

Deuteronomy 32:39 (NASB)

³⁹ See now that I, I am He,
And there is no god besides Me;
It is I *who* put to death and give life.
I have wounded and *it is* I *who* heal,
and there is no one who can save
anyone from My hand.

Isaiah 45:5-7 (NASB)

⁵ I am the LORD (יְהֹוָה - *YEHOVAH*), and **there is no one else**;
There is no GOD except Me.
I will arm you, though you have not known Me,
⁶ So that *people* may know from the rising to the setting
of the sun that **there is no one besides Me**.
I am the LORD (יְהֹוָה - *YEHOVAH*), and **there is no one else**,
⁷ The One forming light and creating darkness,
causing well-being and creating disaster;
I am the LORD (יְהֹוָה - *YEHOVAH*) **who does all these things.**

[*see Addendum* – 1]

1 Timothy 1:17 (NASB)

¹⁷ Now to **The King** (*of the Universe*) eternal, immortal, invisible,
the **only GOD**, *be* honor and glory forever and ever. Amen.

John 17:3 (NASB)

³ And this is **Eternal Life**,

    that they may know You,
    The Only True GOD,
    and Jesus Christ whom
    You have sent.

Once again, we see.

    When you have developed a **Life-Style**,

        where you **truly** know and serve **GOD** and **His Son***!*

        You will then have reached a point,

            where **you** and your **Life-Style**,

                will truly **endure forever***!*

                    When you are given,

                        Eternal Life*!*

Is Jesus Really - The Prince of Peace?

Most Christians believe that Jesus is the Prince of Peace! And therefore, much (*but not all*) of their Religious Beliefs, as well as their Church's Christian Theology has been built in large part on this Doctrine.

So, how have they come to this conclusion?

And what are their Biblical foundations for this?

There is only one place in the Bible that uses the term **PRINCE OF PEACE**. That is in the book of Isaiah, in the ninth chapter and the sixth verse.

> **Isaiah 9:6** (NASB)
> ⁶ For a child will be born to us, a son will be given to us; and the government will rest on His shoulders; and His name will be called Wonderful Counselor, Mighty GOD, Eternal Father, **Prince of Peace**.

People have built substantial amounts of their Christian (*and Messianic-Christian*) Theology around this verse in Isaiah. Yet, most of them totally overlook the **PROCLAMATION OF JESUS** in Matthew 10:34-36, where Jesus makes a declaration to **THE CONTRARY**!

> **Jesus** said in **Matthew 10:34-36** (NASB)
> ³⁴ **"Do not think that I came to bring peace** on the earth; I did not come to bring peace, but a sword.
> ³⁵ For I came to set a man against his father, and a daughter against her mother, and a daughter-in-law against her mother-in-law;
> ³⁶ and a man's enemies will be the members of his household."

If Jesus is not telling the truth about Himself, then He is bearing false witness as to who He really is. Does, or does not, this mean that He would have broken one of the Ten Commandments! If Jesus had, indeed, broken one (*or more*) of **The Laws of GOD**, He would have "**SINNED**"! And if He "**SINNED**", then He would **not** have been a suitable **Sacrifice** for our "**Sins**" on the cross! If Jesus was **not** a suitable sacrifice for "**Sin**", then where does that leave your hope for **Redemption** and **Salvation?**

OOPS !

So, perhaps we need to take a much closer look, at some of the things, in the original text. The first place would logically be, to look at the word that is being translated to English as the word "**Prince**" in Isaiah 9:6. When we check in the Strong's Concordance the word translated as Prince is word 8269, in the Hebrew Dictionary in the back of the Concordance.

> 8269. שׂר **sar**. *sar;* a head person (of any rank or class): - captain (that had rule) chief (captain) general, governor, keeper, lord, ([-task-]) master, prince, ruler, steward. (*from Strong's Concordance*)

Chapter 8 — Is Jesus Really The Prince of Peace?

In the King James Bible this word is also translated as:

caption 125 times	keeper 3 times	master 1 time
chief 33 times	principal 2 times	steward 1 time
ruler 33 times	captain that had rule 1 time	taskmaster 1 time
governor 6 times	general 1 time	
chief captain 3 times	lord 1 time	

This raises a question as to whether **"Prince"** is, or is not, the appropriate translation for this word?

Isaiah 9:6 (NASB)
⁶ For a child will be born to us, a son will be given to us; and the government will rest on His shoulders; and **His name** will be called Wonderful Counselor, Mighty GOD, Eternal Father, **Prince of Peace**.

If we back up to the middle of the verse where it says **"His name"**. We may be surprised by some additional questions that arise. Concerning what would appear to be a rather straight-forward use of **"His name"**. However, it's not quite that simple. So, bear with me, because the following explanation, can be somewhat involved, in order for us to explain this in some depth.

There is some additional confusion, when you add to this that in both Biblical Hebrew and Modern Hebrew, there is a practice of in-directly referring to **The Name** of GOD, (*in Biblical times the direct usage of His Name,* YeHoVaH ("Jehovah" *in English*) **[see Addendum - 1]** *was also liberally used in Scripture*). However, this practice of in-directly referring to GOD (*as HaShem - which means "The Name" in English*), will cause even more confusion with those who are not familiar with the practice. Unfortunately, this can also lead to an even further **miss**-interpretation of what is being said in Isaiah 9:6. This is quite understandable! This is especially true for Gentiles with little or no Hebrew Language background. Yet biblically, this practice can be traced back to even before the flood. Evidence of this can be seen in one of the names of Noah's three sons; Shem, Ham, and Japheth. Shem שם is the Hebrew word for **"Name"**. So, Shem's name is **"Name"** in Hebrew. **Why?** Why would Noah name his first son **"Name"**? It seems that since Shem was his first-born son, that he had been dedicated to GOD and His service. And since Noah had dedicated him to GOD, and His service, part of this dedication was that Noah had chosen to in-directly name his son after the one to whom he had been dedicated. It is interesting that according to extra-biblical tradition, after the flood Shem became the King of Salem. For several centuries following the flood, he was known for being a "Righteous King" מלכי־צדק "*mal-kee tsek-dek*" or Melchizedek. So even before the flood, we see the practice of occasionally using the word **"שם"** SHEM as an in-direct reference to **The Name of GOD**, already was in existence. Over the centuries, or more accurately over the millenniums, this practice has continued. Whether they used the in-direct reference of **"Name"**, **"His Name"** or **"The Name"** the in-direct reference was and is the same. They are referring to **The Name of GOD**, whether they say:

שם – Shem   which is – **Name**
שמו – Shm-oh   which is – Name His (*or* **His Name**)
השם – Ha-Shem   which is – **The Name**

All three of these are used as in-direct references to **"The Name of GOD"** and thereby to **GOD Himself**!

It was during the development of Rabbinic Hebrew that the use of השם – HaShem became the preferred manner of making this in-direct reference. Being far less likely for the average person to mistakenly think that the reference was being made to some other person, rather than to **ALMIGHTY GOD**. However, during the time of the Prophets the use of שמו (His Name) was the more common way of expressing this in-direct reference.

The next point that needs to be made is with the Hebrew word for called.

The word translated as **"called"** in most English translations in Isaiah 9:6 is ויקרא. Hebrew reads from right to left, so the word ויקרא - the ו is **"and"**, the י is **"he"** and the קרא is **"call, proclaim or preach"**.

ויקרא = and he calls, proclaims or preaches

Keeping these things in mind; if we look at the Hebrew text, how does it alter our understanding of what is being said, in Isaiah chapter nine, verse six?

Isaiah 9:6

כי־ילד ילד־לנו בן נתן־לנו ותהי המשרה על־שכמו ויקרא שמו פלא יועץ אל גבור אבי־עד שר־שלום:

- כי - For
- ילד - child
- ילד - born
- לנו - to us
- בן - son
- נתן - given
- לנו - to us [children of Abraham]
- ותהי - and is, and you are
- המשרה - the office, the government
- על - on
- שכמו - shoulder his
- ויקרא - and he calls, and he preaches, and he proclaims
- שמו - name his (His Name) [The Name of GOD]
- פלא - Wonderful, Marvelous
- יועץ - Counselor
- אל - GOD
- גבור - Mighty
- אבי - Father
- עד - Eternal
- שר - Chief Leader, Supreme Ruler (*not Prince*)
- שלום – peace

It is saying, "For a child born to us, a son; and the office of government is on his shoulders and he (*the son*) calls (*preaches and proclaims*) His Name (The Name of GOD, *to be*) Wonderful, Counselor, Mighty GOD, Eternal Father, The Supreme Ruler of Peace".

In Isaiah chapter nine, we see that in the next verse <u>after verse six</u> that Isaiah goes on to elaborate about the government that will be on the SON'S shoulders.

Isaiah 9:7 (NASB)
⁷ There will be no end to the increase of *His* government or of peace,
On the throne of David and over His kingdom,
To establish it and to uphold it with justice and righteousness
From then on and forevermore.
The zeal of the **LORD of host** will accomplish this.

Notice: it is the **LORD of host** that accomplishes the peace and establishes the government. Because after GOD establishes the government and the peace that goes with it. Then it is GOD who places the government on the **Son's** shoulders. It is not the **SON** who does it*!*

Because the Son has proclaimed, **His Name** (*The Name of GOD*) to be **Wonderful Counselor, Mighty GOD, Eternal Father, The Supreme Ruler of Peace.** As well as doing everything else that was expected of The Son. He (*The Son*) is then to be given His reward.

As we looked at this once before, in an earlier chapter, when the Son is given His reward.

Daniel 7:13-14 (NASB)
¹³ "I kept looking in the night visions,
And behold, with the clouds of heaven
One like the **Son of Man** was coming,
And He came up to the **Ancient of Days**
And was presented before Him (*the Ancient of Days*).
¹⁴ "And to Him (*the Son of Man*) was given (*by the Ancient of Days*)
Dominion, Glory and a Kingdom,
That **all the peoples, nations, and men of every language**
Might serve Him.
His dominion is an everlasting dominion
Which will not pass away;
And His Kingdom is one
Which will not be destroyed.

As we have also seen before, in an earlier chapter.

THE ANCIENT OF DAYS, ALMIGHTY GOD, THE KING OF THE UNIVERSE, WHO RULES OVER ALL THE RIGHTEOUS ANGELIC HOST throughout ALL OF THIS UNIVERSE, FROM ONE END OF THE HEAVENS TO THE OTHER; will at that time install THE SON OF MAN as **His** <u>sub-ordinate</u> KING, over all of the inhabitants of **Planet Earth!** Which is a single, small, mostly blue, planet with white clouds, circling an insignificant sun, that is near the edge of the Milky Way Galaxy. Which is only one of the millions of millions of Galaxies in the Universe which **Almighty GOD** rules over.

Our Milky Way Galaxy is itself, made up of millions of different solar systems, of which our sun and its solar system are just one. And when THE SON OF MAN is to be installed by THE ANCIENT OF DAYS as **His** <u>sub-ordinate</u> KING, over the inhabitants of this single solitary planet, upon which we live. He will be placed over all the people of every nation and the men of every language, who are upon this single, small, mostly blue planet, with white clouds, which we know as **Earth!**

And YES! the SON OF MAN will continue to declare, that THE ANCIENT OF DAYS is THE WONDERFUL COUNSELOR, MIGHTY GOD, THE ETERNAL FATHER, - שר שלום - SAR SHALOM!

The Supreme Ruler of Peace

on every **Planet**,

in every **Solar System**,

in all of the countless **Galaxies**,

throughout all of the **Universe!**

The Government is on His Shoulders

Isaiah 9:6-7 (NASB)
⁶ For a child will be born to us, a son will be given to us; and
The Government will rest on His Shoulders;
(*The last half of verse six, has already been explained, in some depth, earlier in Chapter Six of this book!*)

> and His Name (*The Name of GOD*) will be called Wonderful Counselor, Mighty GOD, Eternal Father, **Supreme Ruler** (*NOT Prince*) **of Peace**.

⁷ There will be no end to the increase of *His* government or of peace,
On the throne of David and over his kingdom,
To establish it and to uphold it with justice and righteousness
From then on and forevermore.
The zeal of the **LORD of host** will accomplish this.

Notice, once again: that it is the **LORD of host** that accomplishes this, **not** the SON*!*

No doubt, some are still wondering, how the Government can be on His (*the Son's*) shoulders without the position of Chief (*or Supreme*) Ruler of Peace not also being a part of His position and title? So, how could the Government be on the son's shoulders? Since He (*the Son*) is truly **not** the Chief Leader, Head Government Minister (*of the Universe*). **Nor** is He the Ruler of it, for that is His Father, The Almighty GOD who rules the Universe. Then perhaps in order to understand this better, an analogy or two, will help some comprehend this, a little better.

The first analogy might be where you have an organization and one person is the Vice President, Secretary and Treasurer. It is fairly easy to understand that they are the one who is doing most of the work in the administration of that organization. They are obviously the one who is, out of necessity, exercising most of the authority and power in the organizational government. You could say that the organizational government was on their shoulders. Yet, they are not the supreme authority of the organization. The President of the organization is the head and has overriding authority. Even though it is seldom, if ever used! Especially when the person who is the Vice President, Secretary and Treasure is a competent and trustworthy person.

On a Navy vessel, you have somewhat the same type of thing, which will be used for the second analogy. On a Naval vessel, the Executive Officer may also be the Officer of the Deck at sea, as well as in port. They may also be the Command Duty Officer when in port (*Especially if it is a smaller vessel*). This Executive Officer will out of necessity be exercising more power and authority on a minute-to-minute, hour-to-hour and day-to-day basis than the Captain. One might say that the operations and control, which figuratively speaking, you might say is the operational government of the vessel, is predominately resting on his shoulders. Yet, it is the **Captain** who has the **supreme authority** on the vessel, **NOT** the **Executive Officer***!*

So, even though the ship's GOVERNMENT, so to speak, does predominantly rest on the Executive Officer's shoulders. He is **not** the supreme governmental authority. The Captain has delegated to him the authority to handle most of the governmental administrative needs of the vessel. **However**, this does **not** elevate the Executive Officer to a point where he is the supreme or chief authority! Even though the Executive Officer has great discretion and leeway to act on many, if not most, things on his own, without consulting with the Captain. The Executive Officer's leeway or discretion is **not** total. The Captain has the right and authority to over-rule or change, anything that he, the Captain, wishes to. But because of the Executive Officer's qualifications and his constant effort to coordinate with the Captain, this rarely if ever happens!

Likewise, we see something similar going on in scripture, which appears to be happening between THE ALMIGHTY and THE FIRST OF HIS CREATIONS, the ONE who is being spoken of in Isaiah 9:6, where **The Almighty** places his SON, THE FIRST OF HIS CREATIONS, firmly in charge of the world and places the Government on his shoulders. Yet, **His SON** who has the government on his shoulders, declares his HEAVENLY FATHER to be **far Greater** in all of the following aspects, which are stated in the verse. Just as the Executive Officer of a ship does **not** equal, exceed or surpass his Captain, when the government is placed on his (*the Executive Officer's*) shoulders. So too, **The SON** in Isaiah 9:6 does **not** equal, exceed or surpass his HEAVENLY FATHER!

Hopefully, these examples have given some insight as to how the one prophesied in the verse of Isaiah 9:6; where you have the Government being placed on His (*the Son's*) shoulders; Shows that the Son is obviously **not** the Chief Authority of the Universe!

We have also pointed out earlier. Jesus did **not** have "**All Authority**" until after YEHOVAH (יְהוָה - *Jehovah*) **His Heavenly Father** - **gave it** - to Him! Just as Joseph did **not** have all of the power and authority in Egypt until Pharaoh - **gave it** - to him! Even so, obviously, that did **not** make Joseph, Pharaoh!

We see that **Jesus** (*Yeshua*) is acting in the **Name, Power and Authority** of **His Heavenly Father** (יְהוָה - *YEHOVAH - Jehovah*), to use on His Father's behalf. However, even though **Jesus** (*Yeshua*) has been **given** "**All Power and Authority**", that does **not** make **Jesus** (*Yeshua*) his own **Father**! It does **not** make him GOD Almighty! Even though he is acting with that same **Name, Power and Authority**! Because "**All Authority**" has been **given** to him, to **use**!

We have seen that the Prophesied One, the Messiah, was to preach and uphold ALMIGHTY GOD. And His origin was from before Adam.

> **Micah 5:2** (NASB)
> ² "But as for you Bethlehem Ephrathah,
> too little to be among the clans of Judah
> from you One will go forth for Me to be ruler in Israel
> his goings forth are **from long ago**,
> **From the Days of Eternity**."

Remember, as we have already seen before in this Book. That **He** is **The One** who has gone forth as **The First of The Almighty's creations**.

Proverbs 8:22-31 (NIV)

²² "The LORD <u>brought me forth</u> as the first of His works, before His deeds of old;
²³ I was appointed from eternity, from the beginning, **before the world began**.
²⁴ When there were no oceans, **I was given birth**, when there were no springs abounding with water;
²⁵ <u>before</u> the mountains were settled in place, <u>before</u> the hills, **I was given birth**,
²⁶ <u>before</u> He made the earth or its fields or any of the dust of the world.
²⁷ <u>I was there</u> when He set the heavens in place, when He marked out the horizon on the face of the deep,
²⁸ when He established the clouds above and fixed securely the fountains of the deep,
²⁹ when He gave the sea its boundary so the waters would not overstep His command, and when He marked out the foundations of the earth.
³⁰ Then <u>I was the craftsman</u> **at His side**. I was filled with delight day after day, rejoicing always in His presence,
³¹ rejoicing in His whole world and delighting in mankind."

> The Book of Proverbs is a collection of unrelated proverbs, assembled into a single book. To show where one proverb stops and the next begins, the Hebrew codex used for translating most of the English versions of the Bible, has the Hebrew letter פ placed at the end of a proverbial section to indicate where one stops and the other starts. Proverbs chapter eight has a פ at the end of verse 21 (*just before the beginning of verse 22*) and at the end of verse 31. Showing that it is un-connected and un-related to the proverbs both before it and after it*!*

Isaiah 22:22 (NASB)
²² Then I will put the key of the house of David on **His Shoulder**;
When he opens, no one will shut,
When he shuts, no one will open.

Daniel 2:44 (NASB)
⁴⁴ And in the days of those kings, **The GOD of Heaven** will set up a **Kingdom** which <u>will never be destroyed</u>, and *that* **Kingdom** will not be left for another people; <u>it will crush</u> and <u>put an end</u> to <u>all these</u> (*other*) **Kingdoms**, but it will itself **endure forever**.

Psalm 145:11-13 (NASB)
¹¹ They will speak of the glory of **Your Kingdom**, and talk of **Your Might**,
¹² To make known to the sons of mankind **Your Mighty Acts**, and the glory of the majesty of **Your Kingdom**.
¹³ **Your kingdom** is an **Everlasting Kingdom**, and **Your dominion** *endures* throughout all generations.
The Lord is <u>faithful</u> in **His Words**, and **Holy** in all **His Works**.

Luke 1:32-33 (NASB)

³² **He** will be great and will be called the **Son of the Most High**; and **The Lord GOD** will **give** Him the throne of **His father David**; ³³ and **He** will reign over the house of Jacob **forever**, and **His Kingdom will have no end**."

Daniel 7:14 (NASB)

(*Words in parentheses - were added for clarity*)

¹⁴ "And to Him (*the Son of Man*) **was given** (*by the Ancient of Days*) Dominion, Glory and a **Kingdom**, That **all the peoples, nations, and men of every language** Might serve Him. …

Revelation 11:15 (AMPC)

¹⁵ The seventh angel then blew his trumpet, and there were mighty voices in heaven, shouting, The Dominion (Kingdom, Sovereignty, Rule) of the world has now come into the possession and become **The Kingdom of Our Lord** and of **His Christ**, **The Messiah**, and He shall reign forever and ever (for the eternities of the eternities)!

Revelation 12:10 (AMPC)

¹⁰ Then I heard a strong loud voice in heaven, saying, Now it has come—The Salvation and The Power and **The Kingdom** (The Dominion, The Reign) **of Our GOD**, and The Power (The Sovereignty, The Authority) of **His Christ**, **The Messiah**; for the **accuser of our brethren**, he who keeps bringing before our GOD charges against them day and night, **has been cast out**!

Revelation 7:9-10 (AMPC)

⁹ After this I looked and a vast host appeared which no one could count, [gathered out] of **every nation**, from **all tribes** and **peoples** and **languages**. These stood before the throne and before **The Lamb**; they were attired in **White Robes**, with palm branches in their hands. ¹⁰ In loud voice they cried, saying,

Our Salvation is due to our GOD,

Who is seated on the throne,

and to **The Lamb** at his righthand

To Them we owe **Our Deliverance**!

Immanuel and Righteous Branch

Next: We will take a look at the passage of Scripture in **Isaiah 7:14.**

Some, and perhaps even most, may ask; "But, doesn't it say in Isaiah 7:14 that he is Immanuel 'GOD with us'?" And how can this be, if **ALMIGHTY GOD** created him, to be His Son?

It seems that this might be a good time to take a look at this? We need to look at how the ramifications of this miss-understanding have affected Christian Doctrine. Thinking that it is saying, that Jesus is "IMMANUEL" 'GOD with us', and how this has affected Gentile Christianity. We see that from its earliest times, through the centuries and even today. And because of the influence of Gentile Christianity, this miss-understanding has even had an effect, even on most of the New and Modern forms of the Messianic Movements of today, as well. **However**, the Original Messianic Movement (*in the New Testament*), had no such miss-understanding or confusion on this point, whatsoever. As was just pointed out, most of today's Gentile Christianity, as well as many, if not most, of those in the New Modern Messianic Movements of today, have based many fundamental portions of their theology on this (*as well as other Christian miss-interpretations of Scripture*).

So, let's take a look at this dilemma and see how it might be explained or at least understood a little better.

Matthew 1:21-24 (NASB)
²¹ "And she will bear a Son; and you shall call His name Jesus, for it is He who will save His people from sin."
²² Now all this took place that what was spoken by the Lord through the prophet might be fulfilled, saying,
²³ "Behold, the virgin shall be with child, and shall bear a Son, and they shall call His name Immanuel," which translated means, "GOD with us."

Many Christians will go into how the original Greek in these verses means this or that. But the important thing is that the prophecy, which is being referred to here, and is said to be being fulfilled, was given in Hebrew, not Greek.

Isaiah 7:14 (NIV)
¹⁴ "Therefore, the Lord Himself will give you a sign: The virgin will be with child and will give birth to a son, and will call him Immanuel."

Notice: it does **not** say, "he is" Immanuel, but rather it is saying, "**will call him**". **Why?** Is there something else here that is **not** readily apparent? If Strong's Concordance is checked, it shows that the root word is #7121 קרא which is the Hebrew word used for **"call, declare, call-out,** (*to call-out what is written*) **to read, to preach, or to proclaim"**. What Strong's does **not** show

Chapter 10 — Immanuel and Righteous Branch

(*because it only shows the root word*) is any prefixes or suffixes. Not only does Hebrew sometimes have prefixes and suffixes that are somewhat similar to those in English. But also, in Hebrew, there are some prefixes and suffixes, which in English would be free-standing and separate words. In this case, there is a suffix on this root word in the original text. This suffix is ת. Remember Hebrew reads the opposite direction from English. So, with the suffix added to the Hebrew word it is קראת. It can be translated as **"call you"** *or* **"you call"**, **"declare you"** *or* **"you declare"**, **"call-out you"** *or* **"you call-out"**, **"preach you"** *or* **"you preach"**, **"proclaim you"** *or* **"you proclaim"**.

As was pointed out in a previous chapter. There can be some additional confusion when you add to this that in both Biblical Hebrew and Modern Hebrew, there is a practice of in-directly referring to **The Name of GOD**, (*in Biblical times they would refer to GOD both directly by His Name YeHoVaH (*"Jehovah" in English*)* [*see Addendum – 1*] *as well as making in-direct references to GOD and His Name*). Frequently this practice of in-directly referring to GOD will cause even more confusion with those who are not familiar with the practice, as we said in a previous chapter. Unfortunately, this can and frequently does, also lead to an even further degree of miss-interpretation of what is being said. This is quite understandable! This is especially true for Gentiles with little or no Hebrew Language background. As we continue to review what was pointed out in an earlier chapter. Biblically this practice can be traced back to even before the flood. Evidence of this can be seen in one of the names of Noah's three sons; Shem, Ham and Japheth. Shem שם is the Hebrew word for **"Name"**. So, Shem's name is **"Name"** in Hebrew. **Why?** Why would Noah name his first son **"Name"**? It seems that since Shem was his (*first -begotten*) first-born son, that he had been dedicated to GOD and His service. Since Noah had chosen to dedicate him to GOD, and His service. Part of this dedication was that Noah had chosen to in-directly name his son after the one to whom he had been dedicated. It is interesting that according to extra-biblical tradition, after the flood Shem became the King of Salem. For several centuries following the flood, he was known for being a "Righteous King" מלכי-צדק "*mal-kee tsek-dek*" or Melchizedek. So even before the flood, the practice of occasionally using the word **"שם"** SHEM as an in-direct reference to **The Name of GOD,** already was in existence. Over the centuries, or more accurately over the millenniums, this practice has continued. Whether they used the in-direct reference of **"Name"**, **"His Name"** or **"The Name"** the in-direct reference is the same. They are referring to **The Name of GOD**, whether they say:

- שם – Shem which is – **Name**
- שמו – Shm-oh which is – Name His (*or* **His Name**)
- השם – Ha-Shem which is – **The Name**

All three of these are used as in-direct references to **"The Name of GOD"** and thereby to **GOD Himself***!*

During the development of Rabbinic Hebrew, the use of השם – HaShem (*Thee Name*) became the preferred manner of making this in-direct reference. Being far less likely for the average person to mistakenly think the reference was being made to some other person, rather than to **ALMIGHTY GOD. However,** during the time of the Prophets, the use of שמו (*His Name*) was the more common way of expressing this in-direct reference.

So, why is this being pointed out again, in this chapter, one might be asking themselves? It is because, the use of an in-direct reference to **"GOD's Name"**, along with the use of the word translated as **"called"**, plays an extremely important role in understanding Isaiah 7:14.

Chapter 10 — Immanuel and Righteous Branch

As was discussed earlier, the word translated as **"call"** in most English translations in Isaiah 7:14 is וקראת - the ו is **"and"**, the קרא is **"call, proclaim or preach"**, the ת is the second person **"you"**. The vowels were not yet, being written in Hebrew when the Bible was written. So, another question is - Which way should this word be vowel-ized to show its original intent?

וְקָרָאת = vkarat   and call you (*feminine*) *or* and you (*in the feminine*) call, proclaim, preach

וְקָרָאתָ = vkarata   and call you (*masculine*) *or* and you (*in the masculine*) call, proclaim, preach

Isaiah 7:14 (NASB)
¹⁴ "Therefore the LORD Himself will give you a sign:
Behold a virgin will be with child and bear a son,
and she will call His name Immanuel."

Isaiah 7:14
לכן יתן אדני הוא לכם אות הנה העלמה הרה וילדת בן וקראת שמו עמנו-אל:

לכן - Therefore
יתן - he give(*s*)
אדני - Lord
הוא - he
לכם - to you
אות - sign
הנה - behold
העלמה - the maiden
הרה - conceive (*be pregnant*)
וילדת - and birthed
בן - son
וקראת - and call you, *or* <u>and you call</u>, *or* and you proclaim, *or* and you preach
שמו - name his (*or* <u>His Name</u>) [Name of GOD – YeHoVaH, "Jehovah" in English]
עמנו - with us [the children of Abraham, Isaac and Jacob?]
אל - GOD

It is saying, "Therefore He the Lord gives to you a sign, 'Behold the maiden conceives and births a son, and you (*in the masculine - referring to the son*) call (*preach and proclaim*) His Name (*YeHoVaH - Jehovah*) (*who is*) with us (*the children of Abraham, Isaac and Jacob*) as GOD' ".

This son who is born to the maiden is **not** being called GOD*!*

But rather, He (*the Son*) shall <u>preach</u> and <u>proclaim</u> GOD*!*

Chapter 10 — Immanuel and Righteous Branch

The word העלמה the maiden means a young girl and implies a virgin. Since numerous young girls have conceived and become pregnant each and every day since this prophecy was given. The only way that it could ever be a sign, is for the implied secondary meaning of virgin, to be playing a pivotal role in the original intent of this prophecy.

Some may ask: "Well what about, what it is saying in Jeremiah 23:5-6"?

Jeremiah 23:5-6 (NASB)
⁵ "Behold, the days are coming," declares the LORD,
"When I shall raise up for David a **righteous Branch**;
And He will reign as king and act wisely
And do justice and righteousness in the land.
⁶ "In His days Judah will be saved,
And Israel will dwell securely;
And this is His name by which He will be called,
The LORD our righteousness.

The verse with the question in its translation is verse six. To be more precise, the last half of the verse is where the question is.

⁶ "In His days Judah will be saved,
And Israel will dwell securely;
And this is His name by which He will be called,
The LORD our righteousness.

Jeremiah 23:6

בימיו תושע יהודה וישראל ישכן לבטח וזה־שמו אשר־יקראו יהוה צרקנו:

- בימיו - in day his *or* in his day
- תושע - you will be saved
- יהודה - Judah
- וישראל - and Israel
- ישכן - he dwells (*he refers to all of Israel, probably including Judah*)
- לבטח - to *or* at, safety *or* security
- וזה - and this *or* and this is
- שמו - name his *or* His Name (*Name of GOD – YeHoVaH "Jehovah" in English*)
- אשר - which
- יקראו - he calls him *or* he (*the Branch of David*) calls Him (*referring to GOD*)
- יהוה - YeHoVaH (*"Jehovah" in English*)
- צרקנו - righteousness ours *or* our righteousness

The Scripture verse in Jeremiah 23:6 is saying:

In his day (*the Branches' day*) Judah will be saved and Israel will dwell securely; and this is His Name which he (*the Branch*) calls Him (*calls GOD*), Jehovah (YeHoVaH) our righteousness.

So, we see that Jesus did just as was prophesied. He proclaimed His Father, as our source of righteousness. For He was The One, who provided His Son for a Sacrifice. To take away our sins. By washing us in the Blood of The Lamb slain from the foundation of the World (*Rev. 13:8*). It is through the sacrifice of His Son, that we might become righteous in Almighty GOD's sight.

John 3:16 (NASB)
¹⁶ "For **GOD** so loved the world, that **He** gave **His only** begotten **Son**, that whoever believes in **Him** (*GOD, Jesus or both?*) should not perish, but have **Eternal Life**.

John 17:3 (NASB)
³ And this is **Eternal Life**,

that they may know You,
The Only True GOD,
and Jesus Christ whom
You have sent.

When you have developed a **Life-Style**,

where you **truly** know and serve **GOD** and **His Son**!

You will then have reached a point,

where **you** and your **Life-Style**,

will truly **endure forever**!

When you are given,

Eternal Life!

The First Commandment

Mark 12:28-34 (NASB)

²⁸ One of the scribes came and heard them arguing, and recognizing that He had answered them well, asked Him, **"What commandment is the foremost of all?"**

²⁹ Jesus answered, "The foremost is, 'HEAR, O ISRAEL! THE LORD OUR GOD IS ONE LORD;

³⁰ AND YOU SHALL LOVE THE LORD YOUR GOD WITH ALL YOUR HEART, AND WITH ALL YOUR SOUL, AND WITH ALL YOUR MIND, AND WITH ALL YOUR STRENGTH.' (*Deut. 6:4-5*)

³¹ The second is this, (*Lev.19:18*) 'YOU SHALL LOVE YOUR NEIGHBOR AS YOURSELF.' There is no other commandment greater than these."

³² The scribe said to Him, "Right, Teacher; You have truly stated that **HE IS ONE, AND THERE IS NO ONE ELSE BESIDES HIM;**

³³ **AND TO LOVE HIM WITH ALL THE HEART AND WITH ALL THE UNDERSTANDING AND WITH ALL THE STRENGTH, AND TO LOVE ONE'S NEIGHBOR AS HIMSELF,** is much more than all burnt offerings and sacrifices."

³⁴ When Jesus saw that he had answered intelligently, He said to him, "You are not far from **The Kingdom of GOD**." After that, no one would venture to ask Him any more questions.

This man understood that these two commandments were the foundation for which GOD used to base the Ten Commandments on. In turn these Ten Commandments that GOD had written with His own hand on the tablets of stone, that were given to Moses on Mount Sinai. Were the foundation for all of the rest of God's Laws.

So, what was the First one of the Ten Commandments, that GOD wrote with His own hand on the tablet of Stone.

Exodus 20:2-3

אָנֹכִי **יְהוָה** אֱלֹהֶיךָ, אֲשֶׁר הוֹצֵאתִיךָ מֵאֶרֶץ מִצְרַיִם מִבֵּית עֲבָדִים: לֹא-יִהְיֶה לְךָ אֱלֹהִים אֲחֵרִים, עַל-פָּנָי.

I am **YEHOVAH** (Jehovah) your GOD, who brought you out of the land of Egypt, out of the house of bondage. You shall have **NO** other gods, to My Face.

Chapter 11 — The First Commandment

Later in the Book of Deuteronomy we see the same Ten Commandments. And the First Commandment has not changed, it is still the same.

Deuteronomy 5:6-7

אָנֹכִי יְהוָה אֱלֹהֶיךָ, אֲשֶׁר הוֹצֵאתִיךָ מֵאֶרֶץ מִצְרַיִם מִבֵּית עֲבָדִים:
לֹא-יִהְיֶה לְךָ אֱלֹהִים אֲחֵרִים, עַל-פָּנָי.

I am **YEHOVAH** (Jehovah) your GOD, who brought you out of the land of Egypt, out of the house of bondage. You shall have **NO** other gods, to My Face.

Notice: It does not matter whether or not the other god, is or is not, a **real** Deity!

And so: The Deity of Jesus would **not** give anyone an exemption to the **Commandment**!

Question: When someone worships **Jesus** (*Yeshua*) instead of, or along with, Almighty GOD, The Heavenly Father, יְהוָה **YEHOVAH** (*Jehovah*). Are they, or are they not, breaking **The First Commandment?**

A quick review, from an earlier chapter, on the importance that GOD places on is Son.

Psalm 2 (LITV)
(Jay P. Green's Literal Translation 1993)

¹ Why have the nations raged and the peoples are meditating on vanity?

² The kings of the earth set themselves; yea, the rulers have plotted together against Jehovah (*YEHOVAH*) and His anointed, saying,

³ We will break their bands (*of restraint*) in two, and throw off their cords (*of control*) from us.

⁴ He who sits in the heavens shall laugh; Jehovah (*YEHOVAH*) shall mock at them.

⁵ Then He will speak to them in His anger, and He will terrify them in His wrath;

⁶ Yea, I have set My king on My holy mount, on Zion.

⁷ (*The King*) I will declare concerning the statute of Jehovah (*YEHOVAH*): He said to Me, You are My Son. Today I have begotten You.

⁸ Ask of Me, and I will give the nations as Your inheritance; and the uttermost parts of the earth as Your possession.

⁹ You shall break them with a rod of iron; You shall dash them in pieces like a potter's vessel.

¹⁰ Now, then, be wise, O kings; be taught, O judges of the earth:

¹¹ Serve Jehovah (*YEHOVAH*) with fear; yea, rejoice with trembling.

> ¹² Kiss the Son (*pay proper homage to Him*), lest He be angry, and you perish from the way, when His wrath is kindled but a little. Oh, the blessings of all those who flee to Him for refuge!

In verse twelve, we see that Almighty GOD, The Heavenly Father, יְהֹוָה YEHOVAH (*Jehovah*) expects for everyone to give <u>proper honor and respect</u> to **His Son**! Even though, יְהֹוָה YEHOVAH (*Jehovah*), requires us to only worship Him; and **NO** other!

We are to have **NO** other gods!

It does **not** matter whether they are a **real** or **imagined Deity**!

He, <u>alone</u>, is to be the **only GOD** we worship; and **NO** other!

In verse eight, The Heavenly Father, Almighty GOD, יְהֹוָה YEHOVAH (*Jehovah*) tells **His Son**, Jesus *(Yeshua)*; "<u>Ask of Me, and I will give the nations as Your inheritance; and the uttermost parts of the earth as Your possession.</u>"

As we saw, twice in earlier chapters; Daniel was given a vision of when this transpires!

> **Daniel 7:13-14** (NASB)
> ¹³ "I kept looking in the night visions,
> And behold, with the clouds of heaven
> One like the **Son of Man** was coming,
> And He came up to **The Ancient of Days**
> And was presented before Him (*the Ancient of Days*).
> ¹⁴ "And to Him (*the Son of Man*) was given
> (*by the Ancient of Days*) Dominion, Glory and a Kingdom,
> **That all the peoples, nations, and men of every language**
> Might serve Him.
> His dominion is an everlasting dominion
> Which will not pass away;
> And His kingdom is one
> Which will not be destroyed.

As we also pointed out, twice before in earlier chapters.

IT IS THE ANCIENT OF DAYS, ALMIGHTY GOD, THE KING OF THE UNIVERSE, WHO RULES OVER ALL THE RIGHTEOUS ANGELIC HOST throughout ALL OF THIS UNIVERSE, FROM ONE END OF THE HEAVENS TO THE OTHER; who will at that time. Install THE SON OF MAN as His <u>sub-ordinate</u> KING, over all of the inhabitants of **Planet Earth**! Which is a single, small, mostly blue planet with white clouds, circling an insignificant sun, that is near the edge of the Milky Way Galaxy, one of millions of millions of Galaxies in the Universe that **Almighty GOD** rules over.

Chapter 11 — The First Commandment

Our Milky Way Galaxy is itself, made up of millions of different solar systems, of which our sun and its solar system is just one. And when **THE SON OF MAN** is to be installed by **THE ANCIENT OF DAYS** as **His** <u>sub-ordinate</u> **KING**, over the inhabitants of this single, solitary planet, upon which we live. He will be placed over all the people of every nation and the men of every language, who are upon this single, small, mostly blue planet, with white clouds, which we know as **Earth!**

How then does GOD expect us to properly relate to, and with, **His Son?**

When GOD placed David as King over Israel, the people of Israel were to be under the command and authority of David, as the King. But, at the same time, GOD expected all the people of Israel to only worship Him, and **NO** other!

So, when GOD places **His Son**, as King over all the earth. He will expect everyone on earth to give Him all the proper Honor, Loyalty, Respect and Authority, as **His Son** deserves. If not, then they will reap the appropriate consequences.

Jesus (*Yeshua*) has only **One** GOD, **YEHOVAH** (*Jehovah*), who is **THE ANCIENT OF DAYS**; that He Worships and Loves, with **All** of <u>His Heart</u>, **All** of <u>His Soul</u> and **All** of <u>His Might</u> *!*

The First Commandment
(*Exodus 20:2-3*)

> אָנֹכִי **יְהוָה** אֱלֹהֶיךָ, אֲשֶׁר הוֹצֵאתִיךָ מֵאֶרֶץ מִצְרַיִם מִבֵּית עֲבָדִים:
> לֹא-יִהְיֶה לְךָ אֱלֹהִים אֲחֵרִים, עַל-פָּנָי.
>
> I am **YEHOVAH** (Jehovah) your GOD, who brought you out of the land of Egypt, out of the house of bondage. You shall have **NO** other gods, to My Face.

Are you willing to **"<u>Be More Like Jesus</u>"**, THE SON OF MAN;

and have **NO** other gods,

than יְהוָה **YEHOVAH** (*Jehovah*),

The Heavenly Father,

Almighty GOD ? ? ? ? ? ? ? ? ?

To Love GOD!

The Curse of
(Dis-Obedience To)
The Law

When the New Testament speaks of **The Curse of The Law!** Regrettably, most people do not realize, it is only speaking of **Dis-Obedience** (*and/or Rebellion*) concerning **The Law of God**, which have actually caused the **Curse** or **Curses**!

All too often, people forget (*or never understood*) that **Obedience** to **The Law of God**, will bring forth **Great Blessings!**

Blessings for Obedience

Deuteronomy 28:1-19 (NIV)

¹ If you fully **obey** the LORD your GOD and carefully follow all His commands that I give you today, the LORD your GOD will set you high above all the nations on earth.
² All these **blessings** will come on you and accompany you if you **obey** the LORD your GOD:

> ³ You will be **blessed** in the city and **blessed** in the country.
> ⁴ The fruit of your womb will be **blessed**, and the crops of your land and the young of your livestock—the calves of your herds and the lambs of your flocks.
> ⁵ Your basket and your kneading trough will be **blessed**.
> ⁶ You will be **blessed** when you come in and **blessed** when you go out.

⁷ The LORD will grant that the enemies who rise up against you will be defeated before you. They will come at you from one direction but flee from you in seven.
⁸ The LORD will send a **blessing** on your barns and on everything you put your hand to. The LORD your GOD will **bless** you in the land he is giving you.

⁹ The LORD will establish you as his holy people, as he promised you on oath, if you keep the commands of the LORD your GOD and walk in **obedience** to him.

¹⁰ Then all the peoples on earth will see that you are called by the name of the LORD, and they will fear you.

¹¹ The LORD will grant you abundant prosperity—in the fruit of your womb, the young of your livestock and the crops of your ground—in the land he swore to your ancestors to give you.

¹² The LORD will open the heavens, the storehouse of his bounty, to send rain on your land in season and to **bless** all the work of your hands. You will lend to many nations but will borrow from none.

¹³ The LORD will make you the head, not the tail. If you pay attention to the commands of the LORD your GOD that I give you this day and carefully follow them, you will always be at the top, never at the bottom.

Curses for Dis-Obedience

¹⁴ Do not turn aside from any of the commands I give you today, to the right or to the left, following other gods and serving them.

¹⁵ However, **if you do not obey** the LORD your GOD and do not carefully follow all his commands and decrees, I am giving you today, all these **curses** will come on you and overtake you:

> ¹⁶ You will be **cursed** in the city and **cursed** in the country.
> ¹⁷ Your basket and your kneading trough will be **cursed**.
> ¹⁸ The fruit of your womb will be **cursed**, and the crops of your land, and the calves of your herds and the lambs of your flocks.
> ¹⁹ You will be **cursed** when you come in and **cursed** when you go out.

And then GOD goes on to describe a fast number of **additional Curses**. Which will come if they **choose Sin** and **Dis-Obedience**, which we find in verse 20 through verse 68.

Deuteronomy 30:15 (NIV)

¹⁵ See, I set before you today life and prosperity (*for Obedience*), death and destruction (*for Dis-Obedience*).

Deuteronomy 30:19 (NIV)

¹⁹ This day I call the heavens and the earth as witnesses against you that I have set before you life (*for Obedience*) and death (*for Dis-Obedience*), **blessings** (*for Obedience*) and **curses** (*for Dis-Obedience*). Now choose life (*that comes with Obedience*), so that you and your children may live.

Yet, many Pastors, Teachers, and Evangelist preach.

For as many as are of the works of the Law are under a curse!

This is one of the major quotes from scripture that is used by many Christians to support their **anti-Law** theology. This theology asserts (*falsely*), that Galatians 3:10 shows that Christians are not in any way under any obligation to adhere to OLD TESTAMENT LAW.

Galatians 3:10 (NASB)
¹⁰ For as many as are of the works of the Law, are under a curse: for it has been written, "Cursed is everyone who does not continue in all the things having been written in the **BOOK OF THE LAW**, to do them."

Yet, when a person looks at the original Greek Text, they are usually surprised to see that one keyword has been omitted! And when the omitted word is put back in, it totally reverses the meaning of what is being said. (*the following is from J.P. Green's Interlinear of the Bible*)

3745	1063	1537	2041	3551	1526	5259	2671	1526
ὅσοι	γὰρ	ἐξ	ἔργων	νόμου	εἰσίν	ὑπὸ	κατάραν	εἰσίν·
as many as	For	**out**	works	law	are	under	a curse	are

For as many as are **out** (*of the*) works (*of the*) Law, are under a curse:

Strong's Greek lexicon shows that word 1537 ἐξ should be translated as; out, from or out from, or even without. So, if we do not omit this word, it reads as one of the following.

¹⁰ For as many as are **out** of the works of the Law, are under a curse: for it has been written, "**Cursed** is everyone who does not continue in all the things having been written in the **BOOK OF THE LAW**, to do them."

¹⁰ For as many as are **out from** the works of the Law, are under a curse: for it has been written, "**Cursed** is everyone who does not continue in all the things having been written in the **BOOK OF THE LAW**, to do them."

¹⁰ For as many as are **without** the works of the Law, are under a curse: for it has been written, "**Cursed** is everyone who does not continue in all the things having been written in the **BOOK OF THE LAW**, to do them."

Is it possible, that the translators of the New Testament were so indoctrinated with their own Denominational theology? That rather than changing their own theology to match what they found being preached and taught in the New Testament, they instead chose to alter the New Testament to agree with their own theology?

If you believe that the **Scriptures are inerrant** then the question is; "Were the Scriptures **inerrant before** or **after** the Translators omitted the keyword that totally changed the meaning, and reversed how it is perceived by the readers?"

Matthew 5:17-19 (NASB)

17 "Do **not** presume that I came to **abolish** The Law or The Prophets; I did **not** come to **abolish**, but to fulfill.
18 For truly I say to you, until heaven and earth pass away, not the smallest letter or stroke of a letter shall pass from The Law, until all is accomplished! (*In both The Law and The Prophets, this includes The Millenium*)
19 Therefore, whoever nullifies one of the least of these commandments, and teaches others *to do* the same, shall be called least in The Kingdom of Heaven; but whoever keeps and teaches *them*, he shall be called great in The Kingdom of Heaven.

1 John 3:4 (NIV)

4 Everyone who **sins** breaks The Law; in fact, **sin** is **Law**lessness.

Proverbs 28:9 (NASB)

9 One who turns his ear away from listening to The Law, even **his prayer** is an **abomination**.

John 7:49 (NIV)

49 No! But this mob that knows nothing of The Law there is a **curse** on them.

Galatians 3:13 (NASB)

3 Christ redeemed us from **The Curse of The Law**, having become a curse for us—for it is written: "Cursed is everyone who hangs on a tree."

Jesus paid the price for all of their (*and our*) **Dis-Obedience** and sin. Jesus did not remove any of their (*or our*) **Blessings** for **Obedience**. In fact, they were expected to become **Obedient**. For in the **New Covenant**, they were expected to be **Obedient**, to what God was going to be writing **On Their Hearts**.

Jeremiah 31:31-33 (NASB)

31 "Behold, the days are coming," declares the Lord, "when I will make a **New Covenant** with the house of Israel and with the house of Judah,
32 not like the covenant which I made with their fathers in the day I took them by the hand to bring them out of the land of Egypt, My Covenant which they broke, although I was a husband to them," declares the Lord.
33 "But this is the **Covenant** which I will make with the house of Israel after those days," declares the Lord, I will put **My Law** within them, and **on their Heart, I will write it**; and I will be their God, and they shall be My people.

Luke 22:20 (NASB)

20 And in the same way *He took* the cup after they had eaten, saying; "The cup which is poured out for you is The **New Covenant** in My blood."

(*Similar accounts are also in Matthew 26:27-29 & Mark 14:23-25*)

Chapter 12 — The Curse of (*Dis-Obedience To*) The Law

The New Covenant and **The Passover Lamb** are linked. And may or may not go back as far as the Garden of Eden. Scripture speaks of **The Lamb** that was slain from the foundation of the world (*Revelation 13:8*). It appears to go back to **The Lamb** slain, because of the sin of Adam!

The Covenant made with mankind in the Gardon of Eden. Was the blood Covenant of **The Lamb** which was slain from the foundation of the world (*Revelation 13:8*). This was **The Lamb** slain, because of Adam's sin!

A quick review.

Jeremiah 31:31 and 33 (NASB)
³¹ "Behold, the days are coming," declares the Lord, "when I will make a **NEW COVENANT** with the house of Israel and with the house of Judah,

³³ "But this is the Covenant which I will make with the house of Israel after those days," declares the Lord, I will put **My Law** within them, and on their **Heart, I will write it**; and I will be their GOD, and they shall be My people.

If we stop to just ponder and consider what was stated on the previous page, we may well see; just how important the words of Jesus are when He said:

Matthew 5:17-19 (NASB)
¹⁷ "Do **not** presume that I came to **abolish The Law** or **The Prophets**; I did **not** come to **abolish**, but to fulfill.
¹⁸ For truly I say to you, until heaven and earth pass away, not the smallest letter or stroke of a letter shall pass from **The Law**, until all is accomplished! (*In both The Law and The Prophets, this includes The Millenium*)
¹⁹ Therefore, whoever nullifies one of the least of these commandments, and teaches others *to do* the same, shall be called least in **The Kingdom of Heaven**; but whoever keeps and teaches *them*, he shall be called great in **The Kingdom of Heaven**.

Obedience to **The Law** (*of GOD*) brings **only blessings and joy**. It is **only Dis-Obedience** to **The Law** (*of GOD*) that brings **The Curse of The Law** to those who **do not Obey**.

Romans 6:18 (NKJV)
¹⁸ And having been set free from sin (*Dis-Obedience*), you became **slaves** of righteousness (*Obedience*).

Romans 8:2 (NKJV)
² For the law of the Spirit of life in Christ Jesus has made me free from **The Law of Sin and Death** (*Dis-Obedience*).

So, when Jesus delivered us from **The Curse of The Law**. He paid the penalty for our past **Dis-Obedience**. And with this **New** Covenant, **The Law** is now written on our **Heart**, so we have now become **Obedient** to **God's Law**!

Again.

The Curse of (*Dis-Obedience to*) **The Law**, no longer applies to our lives! Because our past sins have been forgiven and we have now become **Obedient** to **The Laws of God**. Which God has now written on our **Heart**, so that we can do all of them, that would apply to us!

(*Some of the Laws are only for women, some only for men, some only for Levites and some only for the High Preast*)

(*Some are only for those who raised livestock, some only for those who tilled the ground - and so on.*)

Acts 21:20 (NASB)
²⁰ … "You see, brother, how many thousands there are among the Jews of those who have believed, and they are all zealous for The Law; …"

(*Because, these New Testament Christian believers, had* **The Law** *written* **on their Hearts** *! ! !*)

Luke 16:17 (NASB)
¹⁷ "But it is easier for heaven and earth to pass away than for one stroke of a letter of The Law to fail."

1st John 3:4 (AMPC)
⁴ Everyone who commits (practices) sin is guilty of Lawlessness; for [that is what] sin is, Lawlessness [the breaking, violating of God's Law by transgression or neglect—being unrestrained and unregulated by His commands and His will].

Hebrews 10:16 (NKJV)
¹⁶ "This *is* The Covenant that I will make with them after those days, says the Lord: I will put My Laws into their hearts, and in their minds, I will write them,"

Hebrews 10:16 (AMPC)
¹⁶ This is the agreement (testament, Covenant) that I will set up *and* conclude with them after those days, says the Lord: I will imprint My Laws upon their hearts, and I will inscribe them on their minds (on their innermost thoughts and understanding),

Hebrews 8:10 (NKJV)
¹⁰ For this *is* The Covenant that I will make with the house of Israel after those days, says the Lord: I will put My Laws in their mind and write them on their hearts, and I will be their God, and they shall be My people.

Hebrews 8:10 (AMPC)

10 For this is **The Covenant** that I will make with the house of Israel after those days, says the Lord: I will imprint **My Laws** upon their minds, even upon their innermost thoughts *and* understanding, and **engrave** them upon their hearts; and I will be their GOD, and they shall be My people.

Jeremiah 31:31 and 33 (NASB)

31 "Behold, the days are coming," declares the Lord, "when I will make a **NEW COVENANT** with the house of Israel and with the house of Judah,

33 "But this is the Covenant which I will make with the house of Israel after those days," declares the Lord, I will put **My Law** within them, and on their **Heart**, **I will write it**; and I will be their GOD, and they shall be My people.

2 Corinthians 3:3 (AMPC)

3 … not written with ink but with [the] Spirit of [the] living God, **not** on tablets of stone **but on tablets of human hearts**.

The Curse of The Law only comes with Dis-Obedience!

The Blessings of The Law comes with their Obedience!

So, will you return to willful **Dis-Obedience?**

And wallow in **The Curse of The Law** again?

Or will you develop a **Life-Style** of **Obedience?**

And receive, **The Blessings of The Law***!*

The Abundant Blessings of GOD*!*

Found in His **New** Covenant

Temple Sacrifice

The practice of **Animal Sacrifices** in the Tabernacle (*which later were moved to the Temple*) was implemented by GOD, as a pivotal part of His Laws. GOD also said that there was to be one set of Laws for both the Israelite and non-Israelite (*for the aliens, strangers, sojourners and others of all the nations*). And He repeats that there is only to be one Law for both Israelites and Gentiles, time and time again in the Five books GOD told Moses to write (*Exodus 12:49, Leviticus 24:22, Numbers 9:14, Numbers 15:15 and 16, as well as in Numbers 15:29*) and other references are made throughout the Tanach or Old Testament.

Most Christians believe that after the Death, burial and resurrection of Jesus, that the requirements for **Animal Sacrifices** stopped. Or at least they think, the Disciples and the other followers of Jesus quit engaging in them. By the day of Pentecost (*when most believed the Church began*) the practice of offering **Animal Sacrifices** was no longer being practiced by the followers of Jesus. At least that is what most Christians believe. Today most Christians think, **Animal Sacrifices** were now finished, and to continue them would be improper*!*

The question is, are they correct*?* After Pentecost did the followers of Jesus quit keeping **GOD's Laws?** Did they believe that Jesus, by fulfilling **The Law**, had somehow abolished **GOD's Laws**, or at least had done away with their obligation to keep them*?* Did they sincerely believe, that because of the Death of Jesus on the Cross, the need for **Animal Sacrifices** had been abolished and/or done away with*?*

If so, wouldn't the New Testament show this*?* Or does it indicate something very different*?* As strange as it may sound to most Christians, it actually does not assert this. On the contrary, it shows that the New Testament believers were still offering **Animal Sacrifices** and keeping the rest of **The Laws of GOD** (*sometimes called The Law of Moses, because GOD transmitted them through him*). As we will see, some 18 to 20 years after the Crucifixion of Jesus, those who had been taught by Jesus in person for years during Jesus's ministry, were still keeping **The Laws of GOD** and offering **Animal Sacrifices**, which are part of **The Laws of GOD**. Jesus had appeared to many of these people after His Resurrection to teach and instruct them on how to proceed. Following His guidance, they were still keeping **The Laws of GOD** and offering **Animal Sacrifices***!* However, some others had been spreading <u>lies</u> about Paul, saying that Paul was telling the Children of Israel who were living among the Gentiles, to no longer keep **GOD's Laws***!*

Acts 21:23-24 (NASV)

[23] "Therefore do this that we tell you. We have four men who are under a vow;
[24] take them and purify yourself along with them, and pay their expenses in order that they may shave their heads; and all will know that there is nothing to the <u>things which they have been told about you, but that you yourself also walk orderly, **keeping The Law**</u>".

We see that Paul had earlier also taken a similar vow, as these four men had.

| Chapter 13 | Temple Sacrifice |

Acts 18:18

(NIV)
¹⁸ … Before he sailed, he had his hair cut off at Cenchrea because of a vow he had taken.

(NASB)
¹⁸ … In Cenchrea he had his hair cut, for he was keeping a vow.

Paul is either starting the vow or he has accidentally been defiled and is renewing or restarting the vow! In Numbers 6:2-21 you will see where the Nazarite vow is set forth, it required the shaving of one's hair is part of the process in order to start or renew the vow. An **Animal Sacrifice** is required to complete the vow, along with shaving his hair once again. Paul is there to offer the appropriate **Animal Sacrifice** for himself, to fulfill his vow. He is also encouraged to pay for, four other Christian Believers to complete their vows as well (*apparently by purchasing the needed Animals, for the Sacrifices, which the others needed to complete their vows*).

So here we have Paul along with the four other, Christian Believers, which he was helping financially, are all in the Temple and in the process of offering the appropriate **Animal Sacrifices**. In the middle of all of this, Paul is arrested and eventually shipped off to Rome.

As was pointed out earlier, many if not most of the believers in Jerusalem had the privilege of being taught by Jesus, face to face, during His ministry. As well as having had the advantage and the blessing of having Jesus appear to them after His Resurrection. To explain what all of this meant and how to proceed in The Faith. These believers **never** stopped keeping **The Laws of GOD** or refrained from offering **Animal Sacrifices** (*while there was still a Temple*), which were required as part of **GOD's Law**!

We have read the following, earlier in another chapter:

Acts 21:20 (NASV)
²⁰ … "You see, brother, how many thousands there are among the Jews of those who have believed, and they are all **zealous for the Law**; …"

So, what did Jesus have to say about **The Laws of GOD**, that were for both the Israelites as well as the Gentiles? Keep in mind that **The Laws of GOD** include the requirements to offer **Animal Sacrifices** on the Altar in front of the Tabernacle or the Temple, which has the Ark of The Covenant in the Holy of Holies. As we review, once again, this declaration of Jesus.

Matthew 5:17-19 (NASB)
¹⁷ "**Do not think that I came to abolish The Law or The Prophets**;
I did not come to abolish but to fulfill.
¹⁸ For truly I say to you, **until heaven and earth pass away**,
not the smallest letter or stroke shall pass from The Law
until all is accomplished. (*The Law and The Prophets, includes The Millenium*)
¹⁹ Whoever then annuls one of the least of these commandments,
and teaches others *to do* the same,
shall be called least in **The Kingdom of Heaven**
but whoever keeps and teaches *them*,
he shall be called great in **The Kingdom of Heaven**.

We know that all has not been accomplished in the Prophets because the prophecies of Jesus's second coming have not yet come to pass, as well as a number of other prophecies that have not yet come to pass either. And as for Heaven and Earth passing away.

Revelation 21:1 (NASB)
¹ Then I saw a new heaven and a new earth; for **the first heaven and the first earth passed away**, and there is no longer *any* sea.

We can see that the Heavens and Earth have not passed away. Which is re-affirmed by the fact that the Seas of the Earth are still here!

Yet many, or even most, Christians believe that the need for **Animal Sacrifices** have been eliminated or done away with. Along with **The Laws of GOD** that instruct His people on When and How, to offer these Sacrifices. It seems that it does not dawn on them, that if they are correct, this would make Jesus (*in Matthew 5:17-19*) a false Prophet and thereby a false Messiah or false Christ.

Oops *!*

If Jesus had, indeed, broken one (*or more*) of **The Laws of GOD**, by giving a false prophecy, He would have **"SINNED"**! And if He **"SINNED"**, then He would **not** have been a suitable **Sacrifice and Substitute** for our **"Sins"** on the cross! If Jesus was **not** a suitable **Sacrifice and Substitute** for **"Sin"**, then where does that leave your hope for **Redemption** and **Salvation**?

This thought seems to never cross their mind. Most of them just keep trying to wiggle around what Jesus said.

Some Christians try to claim that it is only the parts of **The Law,** concerning the Sacrifices that were no longer applicable. But the rest were still in full effect. So, what does the following scripture say about the idea of, only part of **The Law**, that refers to Sacrifices, being nullified?

Deuteronomy 4:2 (NASB)
² You shall **not add** to the word which I am commanding you, **nor take away** from it, that you may keep the commandments of the LORD your GOD which I command you.

Is it possible that somehow, they think that this really does not apply to them? Since they are part of the Church? Besides that's the Old Testament*!* Some of them will say.

We saw earlier what Jesus had to say about **The Laws of GOD** and the books of the Prophets, not losing a single stroke of the pen, in Matthew 5:17-19. Which makes it very interesting as to what he says in the very next verse!

Matthew 5:20 (NASB)
²⁰ "For I say to you that unless your righteousness surpasses *that* of the **Scribes** and **Pharisees**, you will not enter the **Kingdom of Heaven**."

For your own righteousness to surpass that of the Scribes and Pharisees, we must avoid the lack-of-righteousness in which they were engaging in. So, what were the things which they were doing? They were adding all kinds of **do's** and **don'ts**, to **God's Laws**, that **God** never put in the Bible. [*see Addendum - 2*] Dis-regarding most of what they dis-liked. Generally speaking, they added more than they took away. Whereas most Christian Denominations and Churches today tend to take away more than they add. In both cases, each one is both, **adding to** and **taking away** from, **The Laws of God**!

Deuteronomy 12:32 (NASB)
(Deut. 13:1 in the Hebrew text)
³² "Whatever I command you, you shall be careful to do; you shall **not** add to **nor** take away from it."

Deuteronomy 5:32 (NASB)
³² So you shall observe to do just as the LORD your GOD has commanded you; you shall **not** turn aside to the right or to the left.

So, where does this leave all of the Christians, who ardently declare that Jesus's death on the cross, rendered the need of more Animal Sacrifices null and void for all time? Even though, we see in Zechariah 14:16-21 that during the Millennium, when Jesus is ruling in Jerusalem, there will be Animal Sacrifices being offered in the Millennial Temple*!*

Joshua 23:6 (NASB)
⁶ Be very firm, then, to keep and do all that is written in the book of **The Law** of Moses, so that you may **not** turn aside from it to the right hand or to the left,

Joshua 1:7 (NASB)
⁷ Only be strong and very courageous; be careful to do according to all **The Law** which Moses My servant commanded you; do **not** turn from it to the right or to the left, so that you may have success wherever you go.

Pay close attention to what Jesus is saying in the following*!*

Mark 13:14-15 (NASB)
¹⁴ "But when you see the ABOMINATION OF DESOLATION standing where it should not be (let the reader understand), then those who are in Judea must flee to the mountains.
¹⁵ The one who is on the housetop must not go down, or go in to get anything out of his house;

Chapter 13 — Temple Sacrifice

The prophecies in the book of Daniel about the ABOMINATION OF DESOLATION were fulfilled at least in part during the Second Temple era. When the **Second Temple** in Jerusalem was looted, services were stopped, and Judaism was outlawed. In 167 BCE, **Antiochus** ordered for **Zeus** to be worshipped in the Temple in Jerusalem. He also banned circumcision and ordered pigs to be sacrificed at the altar in the Temple.

Jesus is telling us that there will be another fulfillment in the future of these Prophecies, which is to come in the future. Jesus fully recognized that these prophecies had their first fulfillment during the time of the Maccabees. At which time the Maccabees re-took the Temple, through military conquest and rededicated the Temple in Jerusalem; **re-establishing Animal Sacrifices** and the other Offerings. It was at this time, that the festival of Hanukkah began, in order to celebrate the re-Dedication of the Temple (*Hanukkah is the Hebrew word for Dedication*).

Jesus and His disciples appear to have been in the Temple in Jerusalem, in John 10:22, for the purpose of keeping the feast of Hanukkah (*in Hebrew*) or the feast of Dedication (*in English*).

We see Jesus declaring to those who are with Him, in the books of both Mark and Matthew; that there will be another **SECOND** fulfillment of these prophecies in Daniel. Perhaps both a **SECOND** and **THIRD** fulfillment of these prophecies are possible.

Matthew 24:15-18 (NASB)
¹⁵ "Therefore when you see the ABOMINATION OF DESOLATION which was spoken of through Daniel the prophet, standing in the holy place (let the reader understand),
¹⁶ then those who are in Judea must flee to the mountains.
¹⁷ Whoever is on the housetop must not go down to get the things out that are in his house.
¹⁸ Whoever is in the field must not turn back to get his cloak.

Could this possibly be a third fulfillment?

That is yet to happen, in the near future?

After the invention of the **SMARTPHONE**!

Where you can see a televised event, even if you are on your house top, miles away from the Temple. As well as someone else, seeing the same event in a field somewhere else in Judea, again miles and miles away from where the event is actually happening.

Daniel 9:26-27 (NASB)
²⁶ Then after the sixty-two weeks the Messiah will be cut off and have nothing, and the people of the prince who is to come will destroy the city and the sanctuary. And its end *will come* with a flood; even to the end there will be war; desolations are determined.

Chapter 13 — Temple Sacrifice

This appears to be the **second** of three events of which are being referred to in the book of Daniel with the **Messiah** being cut off and the destruction of the **Second Temple**.

> ²⁷ And he will make a firm covenant with the many for one week, but in the middle of the week **he will put a stop to sacrifice and grain offering**; and on the wing of abominations *will come* one who makes desolate, even until a complete destruction, one that is decreed, is poured out on the one who makes desolate."

Most Christians do not realize that they are actually siding with the **Man of Sin** by wanting the Animal Sacrifices to remain halted. As they have been since the destruction of the Second Temple. In the future, it appears that they may well be restarted once again*!* And most Christians, will most likely, want them to be stopped, declaring that Jesus was the final Sacrifice for Sin. If this is true? Then why will Jesus be supervising Animal Sacrifices during the Millennium, in the new rebuilt Millennial Temple (Zechariah 14:16-21)?

> **Daniel 11:31-32** (NASB)
> ³¹ Forces from him will arise, desecrate the sanctuary fortress, and **do away with the regular sacrifice**. And they will set up the ABOMINATION OF DESOLATION.
> ³² By smooth *words* he will turn to godlessness those who act wickedly toward the covenant, but the people who know their GOD will display strength and take action.

This one appears to most likely be referring to the **First** fulfillment. With the people who know their GOD (*the Maccabees*) displaying strength and taking action.

> **Daniel 12:10-12** (NASB)
> ¹⁰ Many will be purged, purified and refined, but the wicked will act wickedly; and none of the wicked will understand, but those who have insight will understand.
> ¹¹ From the time that **the regular sacrifice is abolished** and the Abomination of Desolation is set up, *there will be* 1,290 days.
> ¹² How blessed is he who keeps waiting and attains to the 1,335 days!

Is it possible that this is what is being referred to in Revelation chapter 13 where it talks about forty-two months which, depending on which calendar you use, is approximately 1290 days? It goes on to speak of an image that will be set up and that everyone is told to worship it!

> **Matthew 24:15-18** (NASB)
> ¹⁵ "Therefore when you see the ABOMINATION OF DESOLATION which was spoken of through Daniel the prophet, standing in the holy place (let the reader understand),
> ¹⁶ then those who are in Judea must flee to the mountains.
> ¹⁷ Whoever is on the housetop must not go down to get the things out that are in his house.
> ¹⁸ Whoever is in the field must not turn back to get his cloak.

As pointed out earlier, it appears that this most likely could only happen after the invention of the SMARTPHONE! Where you can see a televised event, wherever you may be. If you are on a house top, miles away from the Temple. Or even in a field somewhere else in Judea, miles and miles away.

Those who rejected the **Animal Sacrifices** before Jesus came, were rejecting that which represented the one who would redeem them from their sins! Whether or not they fully understood what they were doing, they were rejecting Jesus! Those in the Church today who reject the Animal Sacrifices that may well soon start again. Are they or are they not, also rejecting the one whom these Sacrifices represent as well? Just as it will be for all of the Millennium when Jesus rules from Jerusalem and requires the **Animal Sacrifices** to continue (*as a memorial of His Sacrifice*) as He reigns and rules as **KING OF THE EARTH** from Jerusalem (*Zechariah 14:16-21*).

Zechariah 6:12-13 (NASB)

¹² "…, 'Thus says the LORD of host, "Behold, a man whose name is Branch, for He will branch out from where He is; and He will build the Temple of The LORD.
¹³ Yes, it is He who will build the Temple of The LORD, and He who will bear the honor and sit and rule on His throne. Thus, He will be a priest on His throne, and the counsel of peace will be between the two offices."'

Yet today many, if not most, Christians try and add to **GOD's Law** - saying that **GOD** only intended for the **Animal Sacrifices** to be in effect, until the <u>**Redeemer**</u> **of Mankind, HIS SON** would come to die for our sins and redeem us.

Proverbs 30:5-6
Every word of GOD is tested;
He is a shield to those who take refuge in Him.
<u>Do not add to His words</u>
Or He will reprove you,
and you will be proved to be a <u>liar</u>.

Oops!

The Woman caught in Adultery

For centuries many people have been told, **"The only Scriptures you really ever need is the "NEW" Testament.** Figuratively speaking, this is the same as trying to build a house from the roof down. It sounds pretty foolish. *Because whether it is your theology or your house, they both need to be built on a strong and firm foundation*!

Another good analogy could be given between a story in a novel and a story in The Bible. The way some people read or skim through a mystery novel could serve as an appropriate example.

Sometimes a reader gets impatient. They may just scan the pages for clues, to see if they can determine the end before the author reveals it. Most authors will give a number of clues along with the basic storyline in the first few chapters. Then they throw in a lot of vital information and complex details in the middle. Finally, in a good book, the author brings all of those **"LOOSE"** ends together in the last chapter or two. Some readers who don't care for **"MYSTERIES"** get bored with all the details. Sometimes, they will skip over the beginning and the middle of the book (*never mind if they miss the whole point of the story*) and go right to the last chapter. Sadly, some people are arrogant enough to think they can determine the entire plot, from what they read in the last chapter. If the author is any good at all, these poor souls will usually arrive at a totally erroneous conclusion. Instead of outwitting the writer, they may well end up being **"Dead Wrong"** in their theoretical conclusion. These same individuals would probably make derogatory remarks about the book, regardless of how good it might have been. The fact that they never bothered to read the whole book in the manner it was intended, couldn't have any bearing on their assessment. Now, could it?

Something similar, all too often, has happened with the Bible, showing how some of the numerous continuing errors concerning **"NEW" Testament** theology, may well have started.

In John Chapter 8 verses 4 through 11, we find one of the places that illustrates how important understanding the **"foundation"** and **"background"** of The Laws of GOD (*sometimes called The Law of Moses, because it was transmitted through him*) really is. In order for us to truly have an accurate understanding of what is actually going on in The New Testament. It seems that nearly every sermon or commentary we have heard or read seems to come to different conclusions as to what is transpiring in this particular part, of the chapter of John. We have yet to find a New Testament theologian that addresses the most important principles of this story. These principles are only to be found in the Old Testament. Perhaps there is someone somewhere who has figured it out, but at the moment (*while this is being written*) we haven't stumbled across him or her.

John 8:4-11 (NASB)

4 They said to Him, "Teacher, this woman has been caught in adultery, in the very act."

Chapter 14 **The Woman Caught In Adultery**

> ⁵ "Now in The Law Moses commanded us to stone such women; what then do You say?"
> ⁶ And they were saying this, <u>**testing Him**</u>**, in order that they might have grounds for** <u>**accusing Him**</u>.
> ⁷ But when they persisted in asking Him, He straightened up, and said to them. "He who is without sin among you, let him be the first to throw a stone at her."
> ⁸ And again, He stooped down, and wrote on the ground.
> ⁹ And when they heard it, they began to go out one by one, beginning with the older ones, and He was left alone, and the woman, where she had been, in the midst.
> ¹⁰ And straightening up, Jesus said to her, "Woman, where are they? Did no one condemn you?"
> ¹¹ And she said, "No one, LORD." And Jesus said, "Neither do I condemn you; go your way. From now on sin no more."

Some study Bibles have footnoted these verses from John as *"Not found in most of the oldest manuscripts"*. Even so, if it is an accurate account, which seems logical. We must look at the passage in light of traditional Biblical Jewish Laws. Individuals, who are not familiar with The Mosaic Laws referred to in this scenario, would not know the **"legal"** procedure required to bring charges for a death penalty offense. If this had been a proper legal proceeding, the following questions would have been addressed:

> Did the accusers follow The Laws of GOD in the manner in which charges were brought against this woman?
>
> Did the accusers claim that they personally caught this woman in the act or did they just claim to have eyewitnesses who would testify to it?
>
> How many witnesses were needed to convict someone of a death penalty sin?
>
> What was a judge required by GOD to do in a court under His Laws?
>
> Did Jesus (*Yeshua*) qualify as a judge under The Law?

These questions would need to be answered before the reader could know for certain whether or not The Law had been broken or upheld by Jesus when He said He did not condemn her. Many people adamantly (*but ignorantly*) proclaim that Jesus broke The Law of GOD by not having the woman stoned. If Jesus had, indeed, broken one of The Laws of God, He would have <u>**"SINNED"**</u>*!* And if He **"SINNED"**, then He would not have been a suitable **Sacrifice** for our <u>**"Sins" on the cross**</u>*!* If Jesus was not a suitable sacrifice for **"Sin"**, then where does that leave your hope for **Redemption** and **Salvation?**

So, perhaps we need to look a little closer at these passages. Verse six states that the accusers wanted to trap Jesus in order to have grounds for accusing Him. Is it possible, that they

Chapter 14 — The Woman Caught In Adultery

tried to present the case in such a way, that it would not matter whether Jesus agreed or disagreed with them? That they would still have something to accuse Him of? If so, either way they would have had some legal grounds to accuse Him of breaking The Law; or so they thought. The reader can only know this if they are familiar, not only with The Biblical Law, but also the Nature of GOD.

The Law required two or more eyewitnesses (*one - was not enough*) to testify in court before anyone could be put to death. Their testimonies must agree without any significant differences being found. In these verses, we do not see any eyewitnesses being produced, only **"second hand"** testimony.

One other important fact for us to note is that the **"eye"** witnesses were required to be the initial executioners.

Deuteronomy 17:5-7 (NASB)
⁵ then you shall bring out that man or that woman
who has done this evil deed, to your gates,
that is the man or the woman, and you shall stone
them to death.
⁶ "On the **EVIDENCE OF TWO OR THREE WITNESSES**,
he who is to die shall be put to death; **HE SHALL
NOT BE PUT TO DEATH ON THE EVIDENCE OF ONE WITNESS**."
⁷ "**THE HAND OF THE WITNESSES SHALL BE FIRST AGAINST
HIM TO PUT HIM TO DEATH,** and afterwards the hand of all
the people. So, you shall purge the evil from your midst."

Is it possible, the words written in the sand by Jesus pertained to the verses of The Law they were trying to use against Him? Perhaps they were trying to use verse 5 **"out of context"** in order to trick Jesus? It seems very probable that Jesus might have reminded these accusers of the scriptures that immediately followed the legal requirements of verse 5. Pointing out that He was fully aware of verses 6 and 7. As well as verses 8 through 12.

Read carefully:

Deuteronomy 17:8-12 (NASB)
⁸ "If a case is too difficult for you to decide,
between one kind of homicide and another,
between one kind of lawsuit or another, and
between one kind of assault and another,
being cases of dispute in your courts,
then you shall arise and go up to the place
which the LORD your GOD chooses."
⁹ "So, you shall come to the Levitical Priest or
the **Judge** who is in office in those days, and
you shall inquire of them, and they will declare
to you the verdict in the case."
¹⁰ "And you shall do according to the terms
of the verdict which they declare to you from
that place which the LORD chooses; and you

shall be careful to observe according **To All That They Teach You.**

[11] "According to the terms of The Law which they teach you, and according to the verdict which they tell you, and you shall do; **You Shall Not Turn Aside From The Word Which They Declare To You, To The Right Or The Left.**

[12] "And the **Man Who Acts Presumptuously By Not Listening To The Priest Who Stands There To Serve The Lord Your God, Nor To The Judge, That Man Shall Die:** Thus, You Shall Purge The Evil From Israel.

When Jesus asked for those who were without sin in the matter to cast the first stone. He was asking for the **Two or More eyewitnesses** to come forth. (*the following is from J.P. Green's Interlinear of the Bible*)

361	5216	4413	3037	1909	846	906
ο αναμαρτητος	υμων	πρωτος	τον λιθον	επ	αυτην	βαλλετω
the sinless	of you	first	the stone	upon	her	cast

"The sinless of you (*in this matter*) first the stone upon her cast."
or
"Those of you who are without sin (*in this matter*), should cast the first stone at her"

Apparently, there were not any witnesses present (*or at least not two or more*). Realizing they had all violated The Law in the manner that they had brought the woman to Jesus (*as a Judge*), His decision was the only **"Legal"** one possible. Obviously, He knew whether or not she had sinned when He told her to go and sin no more. However, she could **NOT** legally be convicted or condemned to death. So, the charges had to be dropped. This is confirmed in John 8:11 when Jesus said: **"Neither do I condemn you;…"**.

The more one studies all of the factors surrounding this event, the more ridiculous it becomes for anyone to think that Jesus, the Messiah, broke one or more of The Laws of God in this case. When in truth He was actually keeping even the most minute details of God's Law.

This can be seen again, by checking the Concordance and/or Interlinear as to the use of the Greek word translated as **"stone"** in verse 7. He was actually using the requirements found in the Mishna (*the Oral Law*) concerning **"death by stoning"**. The requirements or manner, in which the written Law was traditionally to be carried out. One of these details required the **FIRST STONE** to be a large boulder, too large for one person to lift by himself or herself. Making it necessary to have at least two or three witnesses in order for the **FIRST STONE** to even be lifted off the ground. This large rock was to be dropped on, or thrown at, whoever had been convicted of a death penalty sin.

The word for stone used in John 8:5 by the accusers when it says, **"Now The Law of Moses commanded us to Stone such women;"** is the Greek word λιθοβολείσθαυ meaning "to be stoned". Its root word is λιθοβολίω or **"lithoboleo"** meaning **"casting stone"** which is a stone

Chapter 14 — The Woman Caught In Adultery

that can be held in someone's hand. These were the stones that could be thrown with only one hand. But in verse 7, when Jesus replied, "Those of you who are without sin (*in this matter*), should cast the first stone at her".

The word that Jesus uses for stone here is λίθον or **"lithos"** which means a **"millstone"** or **"large stone"** far too large to be held in only one hand. It is the same word used for the cornerstone of The Temple. As well as would later be used for the stone covering the entrance to the tomb of Jesus (*Yeshua*). This shows that Jesus was calling for the two or more witnesses to step up and pick up the large stone or boulder, which was required to be used for the FIRST STONE. Today some might say it was sort of a *put-up* or *shut-up* statement, knowing that if only one person had caught her in the act of Adultery, there was **not** enough evidence for a "legal" DEATH PENALTY CONVICTION.

When a Judge, even today in our court system determines that there is insufficient evidence for a conviction. The person charged with the crime must be released. Many times, a RIGHTEOUS JUDGE will indicate to the individual that they are aware of their guilt. But because there is insufficient evidence, The Law requires their release. In such cases, frequently the Judge will warn the defendant not to break The Law in the future. Because the next time they may not be so lucky*!*

This appears to be exactly what Jesus did in verse 11, when Jesus told her to, "… go your way. From now on sin no more."*!*

With a clearer understanding of The Laws of GOD concerning evidence and conviction, it is easy to see that the accusers were attempting to **"FRAME"** Jesus (*... in order that they might have grounds for accusing Him. - John 8:6*). If He had authorized her stoning, in the manner they sought, they could have accused Him of an illegal trial and conviction*!* And if Jesus had told them not to stone her, they would accuse Him of failing to keep The Laws of GOD*!* His reply, however destroyed their entire plot by turning their own conspiracy back upon their own heads.

Only when The Law is used properly can its justice truly prevail; the statement in 1st Timothy, chapter one, verse eight, is just as true today, as it was then **"We know that The Law is good, if one uses it properly."** (NIV)

This is only one of many examples in the New Testament, that requires a more in-depth knowledge of the Old Testament (*Tanach*) to properly understand the Biblical background of GOD's Word. Genesis to Malachi, guides and directs accurately, the entire understanding of the New Testament. Who knows how many hundreds of other such examples there are in the New Testament? Most will absolutely require an in-depth foundational knowledge of the Old Testament (*Tanach*) in order for the reader to **accurately** understand what was truly going on throughout the text of the New Testament*!* There is no way that Christians, or anyone else, can correctly understand and follow what was being said and done in the New Testament without FIRST knowing, understanding and applying the Old Testament (*Tanach*) as a reference source, or filter. This is necessary to clearly view the events that unfold within the pages of the New Testament*!* SECONDARILY, any additional pertinent Historical and Religious information and documentation will give further enhancement to everyone's Biblical understanding.

The preceding example has hopefully shown the rewards that come from understanding and **accurately** comprehending the original theology of the New Testament. As well as the original intent which is to be found in this same New Testament. All of which is predicated on **FIRST** having knowledge and understanding of the Old Testament (*Tanach*)*!*

    Making sure that we do have a proper understanding of all pertinent Scriptures before we make any type of dogmatic theological conclusion. As well as any type of Church Doctrine or Tradition.

    So, if you <u>**truly**</u> desire to have a **Life-Style**, that is pleasing to **GOD**.

    Then what kind of **Life-Style** are you going to choose for yourself?

    A **Life-Style** of man-made Church Doctrine and Tradition at its core?

    Or a **Life-Style** of Biblical study,

    with increased insight of Scripture at its core?

    Which one of these will you choose,

    as your own <u>**personal**</u> **Life-Style** ? ? ? ? ? ? ?

How Should We View - The Law?

Perhaps we should first revisit the initial paragraph from chapter one. Where we ask how do we know when we are loving GOD?

How do we know when we are actually loving GOD And not just deceiving ourselves. By only giving lip service to the idea while falsely thinking that our declaration is proof enough for The Almighty? The difference between deceiving ourselves and truly loving GOD is when the central core of our **Life-Style** has become, (*to the best of our GOD given ability*) that we want to obey GOD and serve Him in everything that we do! Since, the central core of our **Life-Style**, has now become **Obedience to GOD**! As we said before; to the best of our GOD given ability. No matter how large or small that ability maybe.

Probably the best answer, on **"How Should We View – The Law?"** is to be found in the Bible itself. One of the most obvious places would be in the Book of Psalms where this topic is addressed in a rather straight forward manner.

Reading through Psalm 119 will help the reader to understand and gain insight, regarding Almighty GOD's Law. This Psalm is an alphabetic acrostic, in which each stanza, containing eight verses, is devoted to each successive letter, in the Hebrew alphabet. Each verse in the individual stanza begins with the same Hebrew letter running in Alphabetical order through each of the different stanzas. Psalm 119 conveys to the reader an enriched and enhanced, understanding of **The Word of GOD**. And how each of us should relate to – **The Law**!

The Psalmist uses a variety of words, (*Word, Statutes, Precepts, Commands, Judgments, Commandments, and so on*) when he is referring to various aspects of **The Law of GOD**!

Psalms 119 (LITV)

 ALEPH

¹ Blessed are they whose ways are blameless, who walk according to **The Law of Jehovah** (*Yehovah*).
² Blessed are they who **keep His Testimonies**, who seek **Him** with their whole heart.
³ They do nothing wrong or evil; they walk in **His Way**.
⁴ You have commanded to carefully **keep Your Precepts**.
⁵ Oh, that my ways were fixed to **keep Your Statutes!**
⁶ Then I shall not be ashamed, when I consider **all Your Commands**.
⁷ I will praise **You** with integrity of heart, as I learn of **Your Righteous Judgments**.
⁸ I will **keep Your Statutes**; **do not** forsake me utterly.

 BET

⁹ How can a young man **keep** his way pure? By living according to **Your Word?**
¹⁰ I have sought **You** with my whole heart; **do not** let me wander from **Your Commandments**.
¹¹ I have hidden **Your Word** in my heart, that I might **not** sin against **You**.

¹² Blessed are you, Oh **Jehovah** *(Yehovah)*; teach me **Your Statutes**.
¹³ With my lips I recount <u>all</u> The Laws that come from Your Mouth.
¹⁴ I have rejoiced in the way of **Your Testimonies,** as one rejoices in great riches.
¹⁵ I will meditate on **Your Precepts** and I will respect **Your Ways**.
¹⁶ I will delight myself in **Your Statutes**; I will not neglect **Your Word**.

ג GIMEL

¹⁷ Deal bountifully with **Your Servant** that I may live, and I will <u>**keep**</u> **Your Word**.
¹⁸ Open my eyes and I will see wonderful things from **Your Law**.
¹⁹ I am a stranger in the earth; hide not **Your Commandments** from me.
²⁰ My soul is consumed with longing for **Your Judgments** in every season.
²¹ You have rebuked the proud, the cursed ones, who go astray from **Your Commandments**.
²² Remove from me reproach and scorn; for I have <u>**kept**</u> **Your Testimonies**.
²³ Even though Princes sit and speaking against me; but **Your Servant** meditates on **Your Laws**.
²⁴ **Your Testimonies** also are my delight and my counselors.

ד DALET

²⁵ My soul clings to the dust; preserve my life according to **Your Word**.
²⁶ I have declared my ways, and **You** answered me; teaching me **Your Statutes**.
²⁷ Make me understand the way of **Your Precepts**, and I will meditate on **Your Wonders**.
²⁸ My soul is weary with grief; lift me up according to **Your Word**.
²⁹ Remove from me the way of lying, and favor me with **Your Law**.
³⁰ I have chosen the way of truth; I have held **Your Judgments** before me;
³¹ I have clung to **Your Testimonies**; O **Jehovah** *(Yehovah)*, <u>**do not**</u> put me to shame.
³² I will run the way of **Your Commands**, for **You** have given me a willing heart.

ה HE

³³ O **Jehovah** *(Yehovah)*, teach me the way of **Your statutes**, and I will <u>**keep**</u> it to the end.
³⁴ Make me understand and I will <u>**keep**</u> **Your Law**, and observe it with the whole heart.
³⁵ Make me walk in the way of **Your Commands**, for in it I delight.
³⁶ Bow my heart to **Your Testimonies**, and not to unjust gain.
³⁷ Turn my eyes from seeing vanity; in **Your Way** give me life.
³⁸ Make **Your Word** sure to **Your Servant**, who is devoted to **Your Fear**.
³⁹ Turn away my shame which I fear; for **Your Judgments** are good.
⁴⁰ Behold, I have longed for **Your Precepts**; grant to me life in **Your Righteousness**.

ו VAV

⁴¹ By Your word, according to **Your Salvation**, let **Your Mercies** come to me, O **Jehovah** *(Yehovah)*.
⁴² And I will answer my reprover a word; for I trust in **Your Word**.
⁴³ And <u>do not</u> take the word of truth completely out of my mouth; for I have hoped in **Your Judgments**.
⁴⁴ And I shall <u>**keep**</u> **Your Law** continually, <u>**forever**</u> and <u>**ever**</u>.
⁴⁵ And I will walk in a wide space, for I <u>**seek**</u> **Your Commands**.
⁴⁶ And I will speak of **Your Testimonies** before kings, and will not be ashamed.
⁴⁷ And I will delight myself in **Your Commandments**, which <u>I have loved</u>.
⁴⁸ And I will lift up my hands to **Your Commandments** that <u>I love</u>; and I will meditate on **Your Statutes**.

ז ZAYIN

⁴⁹ Remember the word to **Your Servant**, on which **You** made me hope.
⁵⁰ This is my comfort in my affliction; for **Your Word** has given me life.
⁵¹ The proud have scorned me utterly; I have not veered from **Your Law**.
⁵² I remembered **Your Judgments** from of old, O **Jehovah** (*Yehovah*), and I take comfort.
⁵³ Hot zeal has seized me because of the wicked forsaking **Your Law**.
⁵⁴ **Your Statutes** have been my songs in the house of my pilgrimages.
⁵⁵ O **Jehovah** (*Yehovah*), I have remembered **Your Name** in the night and have <u>kept</u> **Your Law**.
⁵⁶ This was done to me, because I <u>kept</u> **Your Commandments**.

ח CHET

⁵⁷ **Jehovah** (*Yehovah*) is my portion; I have said to <u>keep</u> **Your Words**.
⁵⁸ I entreated **Your Face** with all my heart; favor me according to **Your Word**.
⁵⁹ I mused (*meditated*) on my ways and turned my feet to **Your Testimonies**.
⁶⁰ I hurried and delayed <u>not</u> to <u>keep</u> **Your Commands**.
⁶¹ The cords of the wicked encircle me; <u>I have not</u> forgotten **Your Law**.
⁶² At halves of the night I will rise to give thanks to **You** because of **Your Righteous Judgments**.
⁶³ I am a companion of all who fear **You**; yea, of those who <u>keep</u> **Your Precepts**.
⁶⁴ O **Jehovah** (*Yehovah*), the earth is full of **Your Mercy**; teach me **Your Statutes**.

ט TET

⁶⁵ You have done good with **Your Servant**, O **Jehovah** (*Yehovah*), by **Your Word**.
⁶⁶ Teach me good judgment and knowledge, for I have believed **Your Commands**.
⁶⁷ Before I was afflicted, I went astray; but now I have <u>kept</u> **Your Word**.
⁶⁸ **You** are good and do good; teach me **Your Statutes**.
⁶⁹ The proud have forged a lie against me; I will <u>keep</u> **Your Precepts** with all my heart.
⁷⁰ Their heart is like fat, without feeling; I delight in **Your Law**.
⁷¹ For my good for me that I was afflicted, to learn **Your Statutes**.
⁷² **The Law** of **Your Mouth** is better to me than thousands in gold and silver.

י YODH

⁷³ **Your Hands** made me and fixed me; give me discernment that I may learn **Your Commands**.
⁷⁴ The ones fearing **You** will see me and rejoice; for I hoped in **Your Word**.
⁷⁵ I know, O **Jehovah** (*Yehovah*), **Your Judgments** are right; and in fidelity **You** afflicted me.
⁷⁶ Please let **Your Mercy** be for my comfort, by **Your Word** to **Your Servant**.
⁷⁷ Let **Your Mercies** come to me that I may live; for **Your Law** is my delight.
⁷⁸ Let the proud be ashamed, for with lies they perverted me; I will muse (*meditate*) on **Your Precepts**.
⁷⁹ Let fearers of **You** turn to me, and knowers of **Your Testimonies**.
⁸⁰ Let my heart be blameless in **Your Statutes**, that I may <u>not</u> be ashamed.

כ KAPH

⁸¹ My soul is being consumed for **Your Salvation**; I hope in **Your Word**.
⁸² My eyes fail for **Your Word**, saying, when will **You** comfort me?
⁸³ For I am like a wineskin in the smoke; <u>**I do not forget**</u> **Your Statutes**.
⁸⁴ As what are the days of **Your Servant**? When will **You** execute judgment on my persecutors?

⁸⁵ The proud have dug pits for me which are not according to **Your Law**.
⁸⁶ All **Your Commands** are faithful; they persecute me with lying; help me!
⁸⁷ In a little they had finished me on earth; but **I did not forsake Your Precepts**.
⁸⁸ Give me life according to **Your Mercy**, and I will **keep** the **Testimonies of Your Mouth**.

ל Lamedh

⁸⁹ **Your Word** is settled in Heaven **forever**, O **Jehovah** (*Yehovah*).
⁹⁰ **Your Fidelity** is to generation and generation; **You** founded the earth, and it stands.
⁹¹ They stand by **Your Judgments** to this day, for all are **Your Servants**.
⁹² If **Your Law** had **not** been my delight, then I had perished in my grief.
⁹³ I will never forget **Your Precepts**; for with them **You** gave me life.
⁹⁴ I am **Yours** save me; for I have sought **Your Precepts**.
⁹⁵ The wicked waited for me, to destroy me; I will muse (*meditate*) on **Your Testimonies**.
⁹⁶ I have seen an end to all perfection; **Your Command** is exceedingly broad.

מ Mem

⁹⁷ Oh how **I love Your Law!** It is my meditation all the day.
⁹⁸ **You** make me wiser than my enemies by **Your Commands**; for they are forever mine.
⁹⁹ I have more wisdom than all my teachers; for **Your Testimonies** are a meditation to me.
¹⁰⁰ I understand more than the aged, for I **keep Your Precepts**.
¹⁰¹ I have kept my feet from every evil way, to **keep Your Word**.
¹⁰² I turned **not** from **Your Judgments**; for **You** have taught me.
¹⁰³ How sweet are **Your Words** to my palate! More than honey to my mouth!
¹⁰⁴ By **Your Precepts** I know; so, then I hate every false way.

נ Nun

¹⁰⁵ **Your Word** is a lamp to my feet and a light to my path.
¹⁰⁶ I have sworn and I rise to it, to **keep Your Righteous Judgments**.
¹⁰⁷ I am greatly afflicted; O **Jehovah** (*Yehovah*), give me life according to **Your Word**.
¹⁰⁸ Please, O **Jehovah** (*Yehovah*), accept the free offering of my mouth, and teach me **Your Judgments**.
¹⁰⁹ My life is in my hand continually, yet **I do not forget Your Law**.
¹¹⁰ The wicked have laid a snare for me; yet **I do not wander** from **Your Precepts**.
¹¹¹ I have inherited **Your Testimonies forever**; for they are the rejoicing of my heart.
¹¹² I have bowed my heart to do **Your Statutes** always to the end.

ס Semech

¹¹³ I hate the halfhearted; but **I love Your Law**.
¹¹⁴ **You** are my covert and my shield; I hope in **Your Word**.
¹¹⁵ Depart from me, O evildoers, for I will **keep** my **GOD's Commands**.
¹¹⁶ Uphold me by **Your Word**, that I may live; and **let me not be ashamed** of my hope.
¹¹⁷ Hold me up and I will be saved; and I will always look to **Your Statutes**.
¹¹⁸ **You** have trampled all who go astray from **Your Statutes** for their deceit is falsehood.
¹¹⁹ As dross **You** have made all the wicked of the earth to cease; so, **I love Your Testimonies**.
¹²⁰ My flesh has shivered because of **Your Fear**; and I have feared **Your Judgments**.

ע AYIN

¹²¹ I have done the just and right thing; **do not** leave me to my oppressors.
¹²² Be surety for **Your Servant** for good; let **not** the proud oppress me.
¹²³ My eyes fail *with longing* for **Your Salvation**, and for the word of **Your Righteousness**.
¹²⁴ Deal with **Your Servant** by **Your Mercy**; and teach me **Your Statutes**.
¹²⁵ I am **Your Servant**; make me consider and I will know **Your Testimonies**.
¹²⁶ It is time for **Jehovah** (*Yehovah*) to work; they have broken **Your Law**.
¹²⁷ So **I have loved Your Commands**, more than gold, even fine gold.
¹²⁸ So I count wholly right all the precepts; I have hated every false way.

פ PE

¹²⁹ **Your Testimonies** are wonderful; so, my soul keeps them.
¹³⁰ The entering of **Your Word** gives light, instructing the simple ones.
¹³¹ I opened my mouth and panted; for I longed for **Your Commands**.
¹³² Turn to me and favor me, as is the way to those who **love Your Name**.
¹³³ Fix my steps in **Your Word**; and let no evil rule over me.
¹³⁴ Redeem me from the oppression of man; and I will **keep** **Your Precepts**.
¹³⁵ Make **Your Face** shine on **Your Servant**, and teach me **Your Statutes**.
¹³⁶ Rivers of waters run down my eyes for **they do not** **keep** **Your Law**.

צ TSADDI

¹³⁷ O **Jehovah** (*Yehovah*), **You** are **Righteous**, and **Your Judgments** right.
¹³⁸ **You** have enjoined **Your Testimonies** as righteous and very faithful.
¹³⁹ My zeal has eaten me up, for my enemies have forgotten **Your Word**.
¹⁴⁰ **Your Word** is pure and **Your Servant loves** it.
¹⁴¹ I am small and despised; **I do not forget Your Precepts**.
¹⁴² **Your Righteousness** is **forever**, and **Your Law** is truth.
¹⁴³ Distress and anguish have found me; **Your Commands** are my delight.
¹⁴⁴ The righteousness of **Your Testimonies** is everlasting; make me know and I will live.

ק QOPH

¹⁴⁵ I cried with my whole heart; O **Jehovah** (*Yehovah*), answer me; I will **keep Your Statutes**.
¹⁴⁶ I cried to **You**; save me and I will **keep Your Testimonies**.
¹⁴⁷ I go before the dawn of day and cry; I hope in **Your Word**.
¹⁴⁸ My eyes go before the night watches, to meditate on **Your Word**.
¹⁴⁹ Hear my voice by **Your Mercy**, O **Jehovah** (*Yehovah*); give me life by **Your Judgment**.
¹⁵⁰ The pursuers of mischief draw near; they are far from **Your Law**.
¹⁵¹ **You** are near, O **Jehovah** (*Yehovah*), and **all Your Commands** are truth.
¹⁵² Of old I have known from **Your Testimonies**, for **You** have founded them **forever**.

ר RESH

¹⁵³ Look on my affliction and deliver me; for **I do not forget Your Law**.
¹⁵⁴ Contend for my cause and redeem me; give me life according to **Your Word**.
¹⁵⁵ Salvation is far from the wicked, for **they do not seek Your Statutes**.
¹⁵⁶ O **Jehovah** (*Yehovah*), **Your Tender** mercies are great; give me life according to **Your Judgments**.

¹⁵⁷ My persecutors and enemies are many; **I do not turn from** Your **Testimonies**.
¹⁵⁸ I saw the traitors and was grieved, because **they did not keep** Your **Word**.
¹⁵⁹ See how **I love** Your **Precepts**, O **Jehovah** (*Yehovah*); give me life according to **Your Mercy**.
¹⁶⁰ The sum of **Your Word** is true; every one of **Your Righteous Judgments** endures **forever**.

 SHIN

¹⁶¹ Princes have persecuted me without cause; but my heart has feared at **Your Word**.
¹⁶² I rejoice at **Your Word**, as one who finds great spoil.
¹⁶³ I hate and despise lying; but **I love** Your **Law**.
¹⁶⁴ I praise **You** seven times a day because of **Your Righteous Judgments**.
¹⁶⁵ Great peace is to those who **love** Your **Law**, and there is no stumbling block to them.
¹⁶⁶ O **Jehovah** (*Yehovah*), I have hoped for **Your Salvation**, and have done **Your Precepts**.
¹⁶⁷ My soul has **kept** Your **Testimonies**, and **I love them** very much;
¹⁶⁸ I have **kept** Your **Commands** and Your **Testimonies**, for all my ways are before **You**.

 TAV

¹⁶⁹ Let my cry come near **You**, O **Jehovah** (*Yehovah*); give me wisdom according to **Your Word**.
¹⁷⁰ Let my prayer come before **You**; deliver me according to **Your Word**.
¹⁷¹ My lips shall pour forth praise when **You** have taught me **Your Statutes**.
¹⁷² My tongue shall answer **Your Word**, for **all** Your **Commands** are **Righteousness**.
¹⁷³ Let Your hand help me; for I have chosen **Your Precepts**.
¹⁷⁴ I have longed for **Your Salvation**, O **Jehovah** (*Yehovah*); and **Your Law** is my delight.
¹⁷⁵ Let my soul live and it will praise **You**; and let **Your Judgments** help me.
¹⁷⁶ I have gone astray like a lost sheep; seek **Your Servant**; for **I do not forget** Your **Commandments**.

As we stated earlier, the Psalmist uses a variety of words, (*Word, Statutes, Precepts, Commands, Judgments, Commandments, and so on*) when he is referring to various aspects of The **Law of GOD**!

Showing us what it **really** means, to have **A Heart for GOD** and its **Life-Style**.

When you have developed such a **Life-Style**,

where you **truly** know and serve **GOD** and **His Son**!

You will then have reached a point,

where your **Life-Style** and,

your **Innermost Being**,

will **truly** know, what it means,

To Love GOD!

With **all** your **Heart**!

The New Covenant

We briefly disgust the New Covenant found in Jeremiah, in chapter ten. Now, we will go into more depth regarding the topic of The New Covenant.

The New Covenant and The Passover Lamb are linked. And may or may not go back as far as the Garden of Eden. Scripture speaks of **The Lamb** that was slain from the foundation of the world (*Revelation 13:8*). It may go back to the **Lamb** slain, because of the sin of Adam*!*

John 1:29 *and* **35-36** (NASB)
²⁹ The next day he (*John the Baptist*) saw Jesus coming to him, and said "Behold, **The Lamb of GOD** who takes away the <u>sin</u> of the world!

³⁵ Again, the next day John was standing with two of his disciples,
³⁶ and he looked upon Jesus as He walked, and said "Behold, **The Lamb of GOD!**"

Luke 22:20 (NASB)
²⁰ And in the same way *He took* the cup after they had eaten, saying; "The cup which is poured out for you is **The NEW COVENANT in My blood.**"
(*Similar accounts are also in Matthew 26:27-29 & Mark 14:23-25*)

The children of Israel were forbidden to consume blood. The only time that they consumed anything that even symbolically represented blood, was during The Passover Seder, where the red wine used in the Seder, was to be a reminder of the blood of The Passover Lamb. That had been placed on the doorposts and lintels of their forefather's homes in Egypt. So, when Jesus said that this is My blood of The New Covenant, Jesus was declaring (*during the Passover Seder – Last Supper*) that He was The Passover Lamb! And that the prophesied New Covenant was in (*or coming from*) His Blood.

Jeremiah 31:31-33 (NASB)
³¹ "Behold, the days are coming," declares the Lord, "when I will make a **NEW COVENANT** with the house of Israel and with the house of Judah,
³² not like the covenant which I made with their fathers in the day I took them by the hand to bring them out of the land of Egypt, My Covenant which they broke, although I was a husband to them," declares the Lord."
³³ "But this is the Covenant which I will make with the house of Israel after those days," declares the Lord, I will put **My Law** within them, <u>and on their</u> <u>Heart,</u> I will write it; and I will be their GOD, and they shall be My people.

Jesus said the **New Covenant** was in (*or coming from*) His Blood. So, the Blood of Jesus as the Passover Lamb, is what GOD is using to put **The LAWS OF GOD** on the hearts of GOD's people! If **The LAWS OF GOD** were abolished or done away with, as many Christians believe, then there would be nothing for the Blood of Jesus, as the Passover Lamb, to place on the hearts of GOD's people! And therefore, there would be **"No"** New Covenant! Since GOD said that the New Covenant required having **The LAWS OF GOD** placed on a person's heart, it is no wonder that Jesus said the following in Matthew chapter seven.

Matthew 7:23 (NASB)
²³ "And then I will declare to them, 'I NEVER KNEW YOU, DEPART FROM ME, YOU WHO PRACTICE **LAW**LESSNESS.'"

The question is: have they or have they **not** had their hearts covered by the **BLOOD OF JESUS**, for Him to say to them: "I NEVER KNEW YOU"? So, then if someone does **not** seek with **All** their Heart, **All** their Soul, **All** their Mind and **All** their Strength, to keep **The Laws** and **Commandments of GOD** (*that would apply to them*) out of love for Almighty GOD then perhaps, The Laws of GOD may **not** have been written on their Hearts?

Matthew 7:13-14 (NASB)
¹³ "Enter by the narrow gate; for the gate is wide, and the way is broad that leads to **destruction**, and many are those who enter by it."
¹⁴ "For the gate is small, and the way is narrow that leads to Life, (*Eternal Life*) and **few are those who find it**."

The Masoretic Text of Hebrew that is used for most of the translations of the Old Testament. Did not have the Hebrew vowels added to the text of the Old Testament, until close to a thousand years (700 to 1000 A.D. or B.C.E) after the New Testament was written. In Jeremiah, the word for New is the Hebrew word חדש when it speaks of the New Covenant. Which could be any of three different words when the vowels are not used. So, let's look again at Jeremiah.

חדש

(*from Strong's Concordance*)

2318. חָדַשׁ **châdash**, *khaw-dash'*; a prim. Root; to *be new*; caus. to *rebuild*:-renew, repair.

2319. חָדָשׁ **châdâsk**, *khaw-dawsh'*; from 2318; *new*:-fresh, new thing.

2320. חֹדֶשׁ **chôdesh**, *kho'-desk*; from 2318; the *new* moon; by impl. a *month*;-month

Jeremiah 31:31-33 (NASB)
³¹ "Behold, the days are coming," declares the Lord, "when I will make a **NEW** (*RE-NEWED*) **COVENANT** with the house of Israel and with the house of Judah,
³² not like the covenant which I made with their fathers in the day I took them by the hand to bring them out of the land of Egypt, My Covenant which they broke, although I was a husband to them," declares the Lord."

Chapter 16 — The New Covenant

What was the Covenant that they broke?

> **Exodus 24:7-8** (NASB)
> ⁷ Then he took the Book of the Covenant and read *it* as the people listened; and they said, "All that the LORD has spoken we will do, and we will be obedient!"
> ⁸ So Moses took the blood and sprinkled *it* on the people, and said, "Behold the **Blood of The Covenant**, which the LORD has made with you in accordance with all these words."

Again, for a second time.

> ³² not like the covenant which I made with their fathers in the day I took them by the hand to bring them out of the land of Egypt, My Covenant which they broke,…

> **Deuteronomy 30:11-16** (NASB)
> ¹¹ "For this commandment which I am commanding you today is **not** too difficult for you, **nor** is it far away.
> ¹² It is not in heaven, that you could say, 'Who will go up to heaven for us and get it for us, and proclaim it to us, so that we may follow it?'
> ¹³ Nor is it beyond the sea, that you could say, 'Who will cross the sea for us and get it for us and proclaim it to us, so that we may follow it?'
> ¹⁴ On the contrary, the word is very near you, in your mouth and in your **heart**, that you may follow it.
> ¹⁵ "See, I have placed before you today life and happiness, and death and adversity,
> ¹⁶ in that I am commanding you today to love the **LORD** your **GOD**, to walk in His ways and to keep His commandments, His statutes, and His judgments, so that you may live and become numerous, and that the LORD your GOD may bless you in the land where you are entering to take possession of it.

Once again, for a third time.

> ³² not like the covenant which I made with their fathers in the day I took them by the hand to bring them out of the land of Egypt, My Covenant which they broke,…

> **Deuteronomy 6:5-6** (NASB)
> ⁵ And you shall love the LORD your GOD with **all your heart** and with **all your soul** and with **all your strength**.
> ⁶ These words, which I am commanding you today, shall be **on** your **heart**.

> ³³ "But this is the (**RE-NEWED**) Covenant which I will make with the house of Israel after those days," declares the Lord, I will put **My Law** within them, and **on their Heart**, I will write it; and I will be their GOD, and they shall be My people.

The Law in the above passage is **TORAH** (Strong's 8451) which is either the name of the first five books of the Bible or the **Set of Laws**, which were to be found in these five books.

Some have tried to say that because the word **Law** is singular that this New Covenant in **Jeremiah 31:33** is referring to Jesus giving us a New Commandment in:

John 13:34 (NASB)
> ³⁴ I am giving you a **New Commandment**, that you love one another; just as I have loved you, that you also love one another

Yet, in the New Testament, this New Covenant is not referred to as a **Law** in the singular. But rather as **Laws** in the plural*!*

Hebrews 8:8 & 10 (NASB)
> ⁸ "Behold, days are coming, says the Lord, when I will bring about a **New** Covenant with the house of Israel and the house of Judah,
>
> ¹⁰ For this is the **Covenant** which I will make with the house of Israel After those days, declares the Lord: I will put **My Laws** into their minds, and write them on their **hearts**.
> And I will be their GOD, and they shall be My people.

Hebrews 10:16 (NASB)
> ¹⁶ "This is the **Covenant** which I will make with them After those days, declares the Lord: I will put **My Laws** upon their hearts, and write them on their mind," *He then says*,
>
> ¹⁷ "And their (*past*) sins and their (*past*) **Law**less deeds I will no longer remember."

If this had been a **new** and **different** Commandment in **John 13:34**, that Jesus was giving to His followers, then He would have committed a sin*!*

Deuteronomy 4:2
> ² "You shall **not** add to the words which I am commanding you, **nor** take away from it, that you may keep the commandments of the Lord your GOD which I command you."

Deuteronomy 12:32 (in most English Text)
(Deuteronomy 13:1 in the Hebrew Text)
> "Whatever I command you, you shall be careful to do; you shall **not** add to **nor** take away from it."

את כל־הדבר אשר אנכי מצוה אתכם אתו תשמרו
לעשות לא־תסף עליו ולא תגרע ממנו

If Jesus had, indeed, broken one of these **Laws of GOD**, by adding to or taking away from, any one of them, He would have **"SINNED"***!* And if He **"SINNED"**, then He would not have been a suitable **Sacrifice** for our **"Sins"** on the cross*!* If Jesus was not a suitable sacrifice for **"Sin"**, then where does that leave your hope for **Redemption** and **Salvation?**

John 13:34-35 (NIV)

³⁴ "A new command I give you: '**Love one another**'. As I have loved you, so you must love one another.
³⁵ By this everyone will know that you are my disciples, if you love one another."

Matthew 22:35-40 (NIV)

³⁵ One of them, an expert in the law, tested him with this question:
³⁶ "Teacher, which is the greatest commandment in the Law?"
³⁷ Jesus replied: "'**Love the Lord your GOD with all your heart and with all your soul and with all your mind.**' (*Deut. 6:5*)
³⁸ This is the first and greatest commandment.
³⁹ And the second is like it: '**Love your neighbor as yourself.**' (*Lev. 19:18*)
⁴⁰ All the Law and the Prophets hang on these two commandments."

Matthew 22:39 (NIV)

³⁹ The second (*commandment*) is like it: '**Love your neighbor as yourself.**'
(*This would include – **Loving one another***)

Jesus is using "one another" as a synonym for "your neighbor".

John 13:34 (NIV)

³⁴ "A new command I give you: '**Love one another**'.

1785	2537	1325	5213	2443	25	240
ἐντολὴν	καινὴν	δίδωμι	ὑμῖν,	ἵνα	ἀγαπᾶτε	ἀλλήλυς.
A comment	A new	I give	you,	that	you love	one another.

(*from J.P. Green's Interlinear*)

The **root word** in Strong's Greek Dictionary for **"A new"** is number *2537* in the above text, is shown below.

> 2537. καινός kainŏs, *kahee-nos'*; of uncert. Affin.; new (espec. in *freshness*; while *3501* is prop. so with respect to age);-new. (*from Strong's Concordance*)

So, we see that the word translated as **"New"** (Strong's - *2537*) would have been more accurately translated as Re-**new**ed or Re-**fresh**ed Commandment.

John 13:34-35 (NIV)

³⁴ "A new (*Re-freshed and Re-newed*) command I give you: '**Love one another**'.
As I have loved you, so you must love one another.

This is **not** a New and Different Commandment, but rather a **re-newed** Commandment.

Remember, that **The New Covenant** can only be given to us, if and when, we have the **Blood of Jesus,** placing **The Laws of GOD,** on **our hearts**!

The Curse of The Law, only comes with **Dis-Obedience** to **The Laws of GOD**!

The Blessings of The Law, (*and the New Covenant*) comes with their **Obedience**!

1 John 3:4 (NIV)
⁴ Everyone who **sins** breaks **The Law**; in fact, **sin** is **Law**lessness.

Matthew 5:17-19 (NASB)
¹⁷ "Do not presume that I came to abolish **The Law** or **The Prophets**; I did not come to abolish, but to fulfill.
¹⁸ For truly I say to you, until heaven and earth pass away, not the smallest letter or stroke of a letter shall pass from **The Law**, until all is accomplished! (*In The Law and The Prophets - includes The Millenium*)
¹⁹ Therefore, whoever nullifies one of the least of these commandments, and teaches others *to do* the same, shall be called least in **The Kingdom of Heaven**; but whoever keeps and teaches *them*, he shall be called great in **The Kingdom of Heaven**.

Acts 21:20 (NASB)
²⁰ And when they heard *about them*, they *began* glorifying GOD; and they said to him, "You see, brother, how many thousands there are among the Jews of those who have believed, and they are **all** zealous for **The Law**;

Because all of these many thousands of Christian believers, had been filled with the Holy Spirit after Pentecost, were blessed by having **The Laws of GOD,** written on **their hearts**! That is why they were all truly zealous when it came to **obeying GOD's Laws**!

The Laws of GOD, through **Jesus's blood**, was now on **their Hearts** (*The New Covenant*).

Luke 22:20 (NASV)
²⁰ And in the same way *He took* the cup after they had eaten, saying, "This cup, which is poured out for you, is The **New Covenant** in **My blood**."

Once again, we see that the Greek word for **"New"** in New Covenant in verses: Luke 22:20, 1 Corinthians 11:25, 2 Corinthians 3:6, Hebrews 8:8, Hebrews 8:13 and Hebrews 9:15 in the Greek lexicon is Strong's *2537*.

> 2537. καινός kainŏs, *kahee-nos';* of uncert. Affin.; new (*espec. in freshness;* while *3501* is prop. so with respect to age);-new. (*from Strong's Concordance*)

Chapter 16 — The New Covenant

Hebrews 12:22-24 (NASV)
²² But you have come to Mount Zion and to the city of the living GOD, the heavenly Jerusalem, and to myriads of angels,
²³ to the general assembly and church of the firstborn who are enrolled in heaven, and to GOD, the Judge of all, and to the spirits of *the* righteous made perfect,
²⁴ and to Jesus, the mediator of a **New** Covenant, and to the sprinkled blood, which speaks better than *the blood* of Abel.

The Greek word for **"New"** in the term **New** Covenant in verse 12:24 of Hebrews is:

> *3501.* νέος **nĕŏs**, *neh'-os;* include. the comp. Νεώτερος **nĕōtĕrŏs**, *neh-o'-ter-os;* a prim. word; *"new"*, i.e. (of persons) *youthful,* or (of things) *fresh;* fig. regenerate:-new, young.
> *(from Strong's Concordance)*

The Covenant which instituted the (*first-begotten*) first-born male child as a priest is what established the first Melchizedek as priest, as well as the one who was to come later, to be a priest after his order, the order of Melchizedek. He is to be a priest forever. (*The second Melchizedek, who is also the second Adam.*) This was **The Covenant** of **The Lamb** that was slain from the foundation of the world (*Rev. 13:8*) was being **"Re-Newed", "Re-Generated" and "Re-freshed"** as **"New"**.

We can see that the first-born of both man and beast, belonged to GOD and were set apart for The Almighty.

Exodus 13:2 & 12 (NASB)
² "Sanctify to Me every firstborn, the firstborn of every womb among the sons of Israel, among people and animals *alike*; it belongs to Me."
¹² you shall devote to the Lord every firstborn of a womb, and every firstborn offspring of an animal that you own; the males belong to the Lord.

We also see that Abel knew of this, after the disaster in the Gardon of Edon. For GOD had already declared that the first-Born, of both man and beast, that opened the womb, were to be Holy and set apart for The Almighty.

Genesis 4:4 (NASB)
⁴ Abel, on his part also brought *an offering,* from the **firstborn** of his flock and from their fat portions. And the Lord had regard for Abel and his offering;

We also see in, Exodus 13:2, Exodus 13:15, Exodus 22:29, Leviticus 27:26, Numbers 3:13, Numbers 18:15-16, Deuteronomy 15:19, the first-Born of both man and beast are Holy to GOD.

Luke 2:23 (NASB)

²³ as it is written in the Law of the Lord: "Every *firstborn* male that opens the womb shall be called holy to the Lord",

Psalm 110 (LITV)
(Jay P. Green's - Literal Translation)

¹ A statement of Jehovah (יְהֹוָה *Yehovah*) to my Lord: "Sit at My right hand, until I place Your enemies as Your footstool."
² Jehovah (יְהֹוָה *Yehovah*) shall send the rod of Your strength out of Zion; rule in the midst of Your enemies.
³ Your people *shall be* willing in the day of Your power; in the majesties of holiness from the womb of the dawn, to You *as* the dew of Your youth.
⁴ Jehovah (יְהֹוָה *Yehovah*) has sworn and will not repent: You *are* a priest forever according to the order of **Melchizedek**.
⁵ The Lord at Your (YEHOVAH'S – JEHOVAH'S) right hand, shatters kings in the day of His anger.
⁶ He shall judge among the nations; He shall fill with dead bodies; He shall shatter chiefs over much land.
⁷ He shall drink out of the brook on the way; therefore, He shall lift up the head.

So, to repeat once again, just so we do not forget. The Covenant which established the (*first-begotten*) first-born son who opened the womb as a priest, was The Covenant of **The Lamb** that was slain from the foundation of the world (*Revelation 13:8*) which is being **Re-Newed**. (**Melchizedek** means, "Righteous King" and was the tidal given to Shem, the (*first-begotten*) first-born son of Noah.) When scripture refers to a priest after the order of Aaron. It is not talking about Aaron, but one who would come after Aaron. So too, when scripture is referring to a priest after the order of **Melchizedek**. It is not talking about (*the first*) **Melchizedek**. It is referring to the one who would come after (*the first*) **Melchizedek** and would be a priest forever. Because otherwise it would just say that he was **Melchizedek** and not point out that he is after the order of **Melchizedek**. We see in Hebrews 7:3 that it is speaking of the first **Melchizedek**. Then transitions in verse four, to the **Son of GOD**, who is a priest forever after the order of **Melchizedek**.

Hebrews 5:6 (NASV)

⁶ just as He also says in another *passage*, "YOU ARE A PRIEST FOREVER ACCORDING TO THE ORDER OF **MELCHIZEDEK**."

Hebrews 5:10 (NASV)

¹⁰ being designated by GOD as High Priest according to the order of **Melchizedek**.

Hebrews 6:20 (NASV)

²⁰ where Jesus has entered as a forerunner for us, having become a high priest forever according to the order of **Melchizedek**.

Remember: After the order of **Melchizedek** goes back to before the flood! The first-born (*first-begotten*) male child, was to be holy to GOD! This Covenant was in effect even before **The Law** that was given at Sinai. Once again, it was only after the disaster with the Golden Calf, that the Levitical priesthood was implemented. Yet, the first-born male child (*who was to be a priest after the order of **Melchizedek***) had to be redeemed by paying Aaron and his sons, to take his place of service to GOD (*Numbers 3:45-51*). If they did not pay to have a son of Aaron (*or one of his male descendance*), to take over his obligation. Then he would still be obligated to be a priest (*after the order of **Melchizedek***). As we pointed out before; **Melchizedek** means, "Righteous King" and was the tital that was later given to Shem after the flood, who was the first-born son of Noah.

The Covenant made with mankind in the Gardon of Edon was, **The Lamb** that was slain from **The Foundation of The World** (*Revelation 13:8*). **The Lamb** slain, because of Adam's sin*!*

Revelation 13:8 (NKJV)
⁸ .... whose names have not been written in the Book of Life of the Lamb slain from the foundation of the world.

Revelation 13:8 (NIV)
⁸ .... all whose names have not been written in the Lamb's book of life, the Lamb who was slain from the creation of the world.

Revelation 13:8 (AMPC)
⁸ .... everyone whose name has not been recorded in the Book of Life of the Lamb that was slain [in sacrifice] from the foundation of the world.

The Lamb's Book of Life was started at **The Foundation of The World**. When names first began to be placed on the pages of **The Book**.

So, do you still think, that the New Covenant is a new and different **Covenant?**

Or do you think, it might be a **re-freshed** and **re-generated** **Covenant?**

That has been **re-newed**.

It appears to have begun with **The Lamb***!*

That was slain from the **Foundation of The World**.

And will continue until **The Earth** passes away.

Then there will be,

A New Heavens and a New Earth?

The Sleep of Death

Psalm 13:3 (KJV)
³ Consider and hear me, O Lord my God: lighten mine eyes, lest I **sleep** the **sleep of death;**

Matthew 27:52 (KJV)
⁵² And the graves were opened; and many bodies of the saints which **slept** arose,

1 Corinthians 15:20 (KJV)
²⁰ But now is Christ risen from the dead, and become the firstfruits of them that **slept**.

1 Kings 2:10 (KJV)
¹⁰ So, David **slept** with his fathers, and was buried in the city of David.

There are also numerous other accounts in both the Old and New Testaments that refer to death as a form of sleep. And because of this, there are those who believe that when someone dies that they have no consciousness, of any sort, until their Resurrection. They believe that when it talks in Scripture of a dead person saying or doing something that it is a Metaphor and not literal.

The question is: Are they right or are they wrong?

Ecclesiastes 12:7 (KJV)
⁷ Then shall the dust (*of man*) return to the earth as it was: and **the spirit** shall return unto God who gave it.

James 2:26 (KJV)
²⁶ For as the body without **the spirit** is dead, so faith without works is dead also.

We see here, as well as in many other places, that the spirit does not die when the body does. When the spirit leaves the body, it then returns to God. So, the next question is: Does the spirit, when it is apart from the body, have any Consciousness or not? Obviously, the body does not have any Consciousness. But what about the Spirit?

When a person sleeps, they dream, whenever they enter a deep sleep called "rem-sleep". They may or may not remember the dream, depending on how quickly they awake. Whether they slowly move to shallower or less deep levels of sleep, before they awake or wake up directly from the "rem-sleep".

In dreams there is a Non-Physicality (*No Physical component to what they are experiencing*) because (*unless they are sleepwalking*) the body is not involved in these dreams; the body is sleeping.

But the mind and spirit are not. There is a degree of consciousness that is still active, in one form or another.

Is it possible that the analogy between death and sleep is also accurate when it comes to the Non-Physicality of the spirit when the body is dead? If so, whatever Consciousness it might have would exist in a form of Non-Physicality, somewhat similar to the Non-Physicality of a dream. This would make the analogy between death and sleep even more accurate than many people may think!

Ezekiel 37:1 (KJV)
¹ The hand of the LORD was upon me, and carried me out **in the spirit** of the LORD, and set me down in the midst of the valley which was full of bones,

Notice, that only his spirit was taken to this place, not his body! And his spirit is still Conscious in its separated state, which is a type or state of Non-Physicality. We see that his spirit still has a form of Consciousness. Even though it is no longer in his body!

Revelation 17:3 (KJV)
³ So, he carried me away **in the spirit** (*again see, that his spirit is out of his body, and his spirit still has Consciousness*) into the wilderness: and I saw a woman sit upon a scarlet-colored beast, full of names of blasphemy, having seven heads and ten horns.

Once again, notice, that when the spirit is taken out of the body, it still has a form of consciousness even in its Non-Physicality, when out of the body.

Revelation 21:10 (KJV)
¹⁰ And he carried me away **in the spirit** (*we once again see, that his spirit is out of his body, and his spirit still has Consciousness*) to a great and high mountain, and showed me that great city, the Holy Jerusalem, descending out of heaven from GOD,

As we saw earlier that the spirit upon death, returns to **The Almighty**. We have also seen that when the spirit of different prophets is out of the body it still has Consciousness, even in its state of Non-Physicality. There is nowhere in scripture, that I am aware of, which says that the spirit loses its Consciousness upon the death of the body. Even though the body does.

Ecclesiastes 12:7 (KJV)
⁷ Then shall the dust (*of man*) return to the earth as it was: and **the spirit** shall <u>return unto GOD</u> who gave it.

Psalm 31:5 (KJV)
⁵ Into thine hand I commit **my spirit**: thou hast redeemed me, O LORD GOD of truth.

Chapter 17 — The Sleep of Death

Luke 23:46 (KJV)

46 And when Jesus had cried with a loud voice, he said, Father, into thy hands I commend **my spirit**: and having said thus, he gave up the ghost (*or spirit*) (*He breathed His last*).

Luke 16:19-31 (NASB)

The Rich Man and Lazarus

19 "Now there was a rich man, and he habitually dressed in purple and fine linen, joyously living in splendor every day.
20 And a poor man named Lazarus was laid at his gate, covered with sores,
21 and longing to be fed with the *crumbs* which were falling from the rich man's table; besides, even the dogs were coming and licking his sores.
22 Now the poor man died and was carried away by the angels to Abraham's bosom; and the rich man also died and was buried.
23 In Hades he lifted up his eyes, being in torment, and saw Abraham far away and Lazarus in his bosom.
24 And he cried out and said, 'Father Abraham, have mercy on me, and send Lazarus so that he may dip the tip of his finger in water and cool off my tongue, for I am in agony in this flame.'
25 But Abraham said, 'Child, remember that during your life you received your good things, and likewise Lazarus bad things; but now he is being comforted here, and you are in agony.
26 And besides all this, between us and you there is a great chasm fixed, so that those who wish to come over from here to you will not be able, and *that* none may cross over from there to us.'
27 And he said, 'Then I beg you, father, that you send him to my father's house—
28 for I have five brothers—in order that he may warn them, so that they will not also come to this place of torment.'
29 But Abraham said, 'They have Moses and the Prophets; let them hear them.'
30 But he said, 'No, father Abraham, but if someone goes to them from the dead, they will repent!'
31 But he said to him, 'If they do not listen to Moses and the Prophets, they will not be persuaded even if someone rises from the dead.'"

When a person has, what is sometimes called, a near-death experience and tells others of it. Many times, people will have skepticism about what the person relates to them, concerning what happened to them. And rightly so! There are at least two or three reasons that many times the stories of different people are not similar. For example, we can use the analogy of two different people traveling by Airplane to a different country at different times. The things that are experienced by one person will not be exactly the same as what the other person experienced. Even though they both went to the same place. One will be impressed by some things and not others. While the other person will be impressed by different things and therefore will tend to remember them instead of the others. One may have spent time in one part of the country, while the other spent time in a different part of the same country. So, when two people have a near-death experience they may or may not, have experienced the exact same circumstances.

The second reason is that The Almighty may have only allowed one individual to remember certain things. Another person may be allowed to remember different things. Because of the intended effects that The Almighty may wish for their memories to have on each one's individual life. One may be given certain experiences which are not given to the other person. Because of a different purpose that The Almighty has in store for the other person. The other person's experience will be tailored just for them.

The third is the possibility of a Satanic Counterfeit. So that when they return, they will think that it is OK to behave in a manner that is **not** quite right! In order to have them tell everyone about their experience. And try to influence them, that it is OK to behave in a manner that is a near-miss and will cause them dismay (*as well as any others they may have influenced*) when they stand before Almighty GOD on the day of judgment, and ask Jesus to intercede for them. As they declare that that He, Jesus, was their Lord during their life, and still is now.

As we have seen several times earlier in this book. Regarding Jesus, being call their Lord.

Matthew 7:21-23 (NASB)

²¹ "Not everyone who says to Me, '**Lord, Lord,**' will enter the kingdom of heaven, but **he who does the will of My Father who is in heaven** *will enter*.
²² Many will say to Me on that day, '**Lord, Lord,**
    did we not prophesy in **Your Name** (*Jesus*),
    and in **Your Name** (*Jesus*) cast out demons,
    and in **Your Name** (*Jesus*) perform many miracles?'
²³ And then I will declare to them, 'I never knew you; DEPART FROM ME, YOU WHO PRACTICE LAWLESSNESS!' (*Dis-obedience*)

Jesus always places the will of His Father above himself. And Jesus will not place anyone's **mis**-guided devotion to Himself above **His Father** or **His Father's** will. In the case above, in Matthew chapter seven, verses twenty-one through twenty-three. It appears that they may have accepted a different (*or Counterfeit*) Jesus? To their dismay and horror!

The possibility of a Satanic Counterfeit, in all aspects of religion and theology, including a Near-Death experience, should never be overlooked. The experience must always fall within the bounds of Scripture and **Obedience** to **Almighty GOD**! Just as with all forms of theology and religion.

However, just because Satan Counterfeits something, does not take away from the real thing that is being Counterfeited! On the contrary, he knows the importance of the real thing and is trying to redirect, as many as he can, away from the real thing! This occurs in all aspects of religion and theology, including Near-Death experiences.

The question is: Does the Near-Death experience of someone (*and its Non-Physicality*) fall within the bounds of Scripture and Obedience to **Almighty GOD, The Heavenly Father?** If so, it may well be real. Even if GOD chooses to sometimes limit a person's memory to just part of the experience while allowing someone else to remember other things.

Yet frequently, some people will think that the experience of one person is not real because it does not match with what others may have experienced. So, some will want to just dis-regard them all. Because GOD did not choose to do it their way. How sad*!*

Most people today are unaware, that it appears that Jesus is making reference to the book of Enoch when He speaks of the place where Lazarus and the Rich Man were taken, which is described in some detail in the book of Enoch. Even though the good place, which Enoch describes, was not yet being referred to as Abraham's bosom, since Abraham had not yet been born. The Book of Enoch also tells us that the Demon Spirits are the Spirits of the Hybrid between the Sons of GOD and human women which occurred in Genesis chapter six. These spirits, for whatever reason, appear to be stuck here on earth, and are not taken by Angels to the same place as Lazarus or the Rich Man, but rather left here on the Earth. These Spirits, like the Spirits of Lazarus and the Rich Man, are Conscious even in their form of Non-Physicality. Which is somewhat similar to a dream when we are asleep! And they crave to have a body, once again, to regain a form of Physicality. If only for a while. As we see in the New Testament, their spirits still have Consciousness, even in their dream like state of Non-Physicality. And they seek to regain a form of Physicality by inhabiting people or even swine.

We have already looked at the account of Lazarus and the Rich Man earlier, from the book of Luke. Now we will look at the accounts of the Demon possessed man and the herd of swine, in the book of Mark (*a similar account can also be found in both Luke and Matthew*).

Mark 5:1-17 (NASB)
The Gerasene Demoniac

¹ They came to the other side of the sea, into the country of the Gerasenes.
² When He got out of the boat, immediately a man from the tombs with an unclean spirit met Him,
³ and he had his dwelling among the tombs. And no one was able to bind him anymore, even with a chain;
⁴ because he had often been bound with shackles and chains, and the chains had been torn apart by him and the shackles broken in pieces, and no one was strong enough to subdue him.
⁵ Constantly, night and day, he was screaming among the tombs and in the mountains, and gashing himself with stones.
⁶ Seeing Jesus from a distance, he ran up and bowed down before Him;
⁷ and shouting with a loud voice, he said, "What business do we have with each other, Jesus, Son of the Most High GOD? I implore You by GOD, do not torment me!"
⁸ For He had been saying to him, "Come out of the man, you unclean spirit!"
⁹ And He was asking him, "What is your name?" And he said to Him, "My name is Legion; for we are many."

¹⁰ And he *began* to implore Him earnestly not to send them out of the country.

¹¹ Now there was a large herd of swine feeding nearby on the mountain.

¹² *The demons* implored Him, saying, "Send us into the swine so that we may enter them."

¹³ Jesus gave them permission. And coming out, the unclean spirits entered the swine; and the herd rushed down the steep bank into the sea, about two thousand *of them*; and they were drowned in the sea.

¹⁴ Their herdsmen ran away and reported it in the city and in the country. And *the people* came to see what it was that had happened.

¹⁵ They came to Jesus and observed the man who had been demon-possessed sitting down, clothed and in his right mind, the very man who had had the "legion"; and they became frightened.

¹⁶ Those who had seen it described to them how it had happened to the demon-possessed man, and *all* about the swine.

¹⁷ And they began to implore Him to leave their region.

Next, we see in the following scripture, it appears that the Angels are allowed a degree of personal discretion in how they interact with humans.

Numbers 22:21-35 (NASB)

²¹ So, Balaam arose in the morning, and saddled his donkey and went with the leaders of Moab.

The Angel and Balaam

²² But GOD was angry because he was going, and the angel of the LORD took his stand in the way as an adversary against him. Now he was riding on his donkey and his two servants were with him.

²³ When the donkey saw the angel of the LORD standing in the way with his drawn sword in his hand, the donkey turned off from the way and went into the field; but Balaam struck the donkey to turn her back into the way.

²⁴ Then the angel of the LORD stood in a narrow path of the vineyards, *with* a wall on this side and a wall on that side.

²⁵ When the donkey saw the angel of the LORD, she pressed herself to the wall and pressed Balaam's foot against the wall, so he struck her again.

²⁶ The angel of the LORD went further, and stood in a narrow place where there was no way to turn to the right hand or the left.

²⁷ When the donkey saw the angel of the LORD, she lay down under Balaam; so, Balaam was angry and struck the donkey with his stick.

> ²⁸ And the LORD opened the mouth of the donkey, and she said to Balaam, "What have I done to you, that you have struck me these three times?"
> ²⁹ Then Balaam said to the donkey, "Because you have made a mockery of me! If there had been a sword in my hand, I would have killed you by now."
> ³⁰ The donkey said to Balaam, "Am I not your donkey on which you have ridden all your life to this day? Have I ever been accustomed to do so to you?" And he said, "No."
> ³¹ Then the LORD opened the eyes of Balaam, and he saw the angel of the LORD standing in the way with his drawn sword in his hand; and he bowed all the way to the ground.
> ³² The angel of the LORD said to him, "Why have you struck your donkey these three times? Behold, I have come out as an adversary, because your way was contrary to me.
> ³³ But the donkey saw me and turned aside from me these three times. If she had not turned aside from me, <u>I would surely have killed you just now</u>, and let her live."
> ³⁴ Balaam said to the angel of the LORD, "I have sinned, for I did not know that you were standing in the way against me. Now then, if it is displeasing to you, I will turn back."
> ³⁵ But the angel of the LORD said to Balaam, "<u>Go with the men</u>, but <u>you shall speak only the word which I tell you</u>." So, Balaam went along with the leaders of Balak.

We see that in verse thirty-three, that the Angel originally intended to kill Balaam. Yet, the Angel had the prerogative to use his own discretion, and do things in a different manner, as we see in verse thirty-five.

It also appears that the Angels may have some discretion as to whether to immediately take the spirit of a dead person to their appointed place or allow them to have a brief time to see what is going on with their family and friends before their spirit is taken to the place where they will await their Resurrection.

After the Resurrection of Jesus, it appears that he took the spirits of those who were in the place where Abraham and Lazarus were, with him, to Heaven. And now, this is where the Angels take those whose spirits are awaiting the First Resurrection. To receive their new bodies.

We have discussed how many believe that after death there is no Consciousness because of the analogy of death and sleep. They believe that after death the next thing we will experience will be awakening at the Resurrection. This is because they forget that when we sleep, we have a Non-Physical Consciousness in dreams, which is somewhat similar to what the spirit experiences when it leaves the body.

Even when the Near-Death experience is real, the person may or may not choose to take to heart, whatever they were shown during the experience. In some cases, they may even tell themselves, after a while, that it was only a Hallucination, or a Dream. In order to excuse certain parts of <u>their own personal</u> **Life-Style**. Because if it was truly real, that would mean that during the rest of their life, they would need to turn to **Almighty God**, with <u>**all**</u> **their heart**, <u>**all**</u> **their soul** and <u>**all**</u> **their might**.

      Making **<u>Obedience</u>** to **Almighty God**

            the very central core

                  of <u>their own personal</u> **Life-Style***!*

Addendums

Addendum – 1 The Name (*of GOD*)

Addendum – 2 The Levan of The Pharisees

Addendum – 3 Works

Addendum – 4 The Law of Sin and Death

Addendum – 5 Paul and The Law

Addendum – 6 The Words of Paul

Addendum – 7 Let Everything Be Established

The Name

The sacred name **Yehovah** (*Jehovah*), derived from the Hebrew יהוה *YHVH*, is found more than 6,800 times in the Old Testament. **Yehovah** (יְהֹוָה *Jehovah*) is "the COVENANT GOD and proper name of the GOD of Israel." Most modern English translations of the Bible, however, use **LORD** or **THE LORD**, in place of **Yehovah** (יְהֹוָה *Jehovah*).

This large number of times that it is used, shows how extremely important, it is to the accurate understanding of the Old Testament text. As well as showing that **Yehovah** (יְהֹוָה *Jehovah*) is more prominent than any other Old Testament subject matter. **Yehovah** (יְהֹוָה *Jehovah*) is the most important word, not only in terms of frequency, but also in terms of what this sacred name represents.

In the Old Testament, **Yehovah** (יְהֹוָה *Jehovah*) is topically greater than any other topic.

Yet, the name of **Yehovah** (יְהֹוָה *Jehovah*), in most modern translations, has been censured and removed, to be replaced (*obscured and camouflaged*) with the term, **LORD** or **THE LORD**.

For example, **Yehovah** (יְהֹוָה *Jehovah*) is replaced by **LORD** or **THE LORD**, in the Pentateuch (Genesis, Exodus, Leviticus, Numbers, and Deuteronomy) 1,820 times. **Yehovah** (יְהֹוָה *Jehovah*) has been replaced with **LORD** or **THE LORD**, 450 times in Isaiah and 695 times in Psalms. Below is a list of the times that the name **Yehovah** (יְהֹוָה *Jehovah*) has been censured and replaced with **LORD** or **THE LORD**.

Genesis - 165	**2 Chronicles** - 384	**Daniel** - 8
Exodus - 398	**Ezra** - 37	**Hosea** - 46
Leviticus - 311	**Nehemiah** - 17	**Joel** - 33
Numbers - 396	**Esther** - 0	**Amos** - 81
Deuteronomy - 550	**Job** - 32	**Obadiah** - 7
Joshua - 224	**Psalms** - 695	**Jonah** - 26
Judges - 175	**Proverbs** - 87	**Micah** - 40
Ruth - 18	**Ecclesiastes** - 0	**Nahum** - 13
1 Samuel - 320	**Song of Solomon** - 0	**Habakkuk** - 13
2 Samuel - 153	**Isaiah** - 450	**Zephaniah** - 34
1 Kings - 257	**Jeremiah** - 726	**Haggai** - 35
2 Kings - 277	**Lamentations** - 32	**Zechariah** - 133
1 Chronicles - 175	**Ezekiel** - 434	**Malachi** - 46

Exodus 20:2-3

[2] I am **Yehovah** (*Jehovah*) **יְהֹוָה** your GOD, who brought you out of the land of Egypt, out of the house of bondage.

אָנֹכִי יְהֹוָה אֱלֹהֶיךָ אֲשֶׁר הוֹצֵאתִיךָ מֵאֶרֶץ מִצְרַיִם מִבֵּית עֲבָדִים:

[3] You shall not have other gods in **MY** presence (to **MY** face).

לֹא יִהְיֶה־לְךָ אֱלֹהִים אֲחֵרִים עַל־פָּנָי:

Wouldn't this include **Jesus** (*Yeshua*) יֵשׁוּעַ ?

Regardless as to **His Deity**;

He is not **Yehovah** (*Jehovah*) יְהֹוָה

who is **His Heavenly Father**

Leaven of the Pharisees and Sadducees

Deuteronomy 12:32 (NASB)
(13:1 in the Hebrew Text)
"Whatever I command you, you shall be careful to do;
you shall **not** add to **nor** take away from it."

Mark 7:5-9 (NASB)
(5) And the Pharisees and the Scribes asked Him, "Why do your disciples not walk according to the tradition of the elders, but eat their bread with impure hands?"
(6) And He said to them, "Rightly did Isaiah prophesy of you hypocrites, as it is written, 'THIS PEOPLE HONORS ME WITH THEIR LIPS, BUT THEIR HEART IS FAR AWAY FROM ME.
(7) BUT IN VAIN DO THEY WORSHIP ME, TEACHINGS AS DOCTRINES THE PRECEPTS OF MEN.'
(8) "Neglecting **The Commandments of God**, you hold to **the traditions of men**."
(9) He was also saying to them: "You nicely set aside
THE COMMANDMENTS OF GOD
in order to keep your traditions!"

Deuteronomy 4:2 (NASB)
² "You shall **not** add to the words which I am commanding you,
nor take away from it, that you may keep the Commandments of
the Lord your God which I command you."

Matthew 16:11-12 (NASB)
¹¹ How *is it that* you do not understand that I did not speak to you about bread? But beware of the **leaven of the Pharisees and Sadducees**."
¹² Then they understood that He did not say to beware of the leaven of bread, but of the **teaching** of the Pharisees and Sadducees.

Matthew 5:17-20 (NIV)
¹⁷ "Do not think that I have came to abolish the Law or the Prophets; I did not come to abolish them, but to fulfill them.
¹⁸ I tell you the truth, I say to you, until heaven and earth disappear, **not** the smallest letter, nor the least stroke of a pen, will by any means disappear from the Law, until everything is accomplished!
(*In the Law and Prophets would include - the Millenium*)
¹⁹ Anyone who breaks one of the least of these commandments, and teaches others *to do* the same will be called least in **The Kingdom of Heaven**, but whoever practices and teaches these commands will be called great in **The Kingdom of Heaven**.
²⁰ "For I tell you that unless your righteousness surpasses that of the Scribes and Pharisees, you will **not** enter **The Kingdom of Heaven**.

Deuteronomy 12:32 (NASB)
(13:1 in the Hebrew Text)
"Whatever I command you, you shall be careful to do;
you shall **not** add to **nor** take away from it."

Matthew 5:48 (NASB)
⁴⁸ Therefore you are to be perfect,
as your heavenly Father is perfect.

Works

Many Christian Pastors, Teachers, Evangelist and so on, will often condemn those who advocate obeying God, claiming that they are trying to earn their salvation through Works! What does Scripture have to say about the topic of **Works**?

James 2:14 (NASB)
(14) What use is it, my brethren, if a man says he has faith,
but he has no **works**? Can that faith save him?

James 2: 20 (NASB)
(20) But are you willing to recognize, you foolish fellow,
that faith without **works** is useless?

James 2: 17 (NASB)
(17) Even so faith, if it has no **works**, is dead, being by itself.

James 2: 24 (NASB)
(24) You see that a man is **justified** by **works**, and not by faith alone.

James 2: 26 (NASB)
(26) For just as the body without the spirit is dead, so also faith without **works** is dead.

1st Timothy 6:18 (NASB)
(18) Instruct them to do good, to be rich in good **works**, to be generous and ready to share,

John 14:12 (NASB)
(12) "**Truly, truly,** I say to you, he who believes in Me, the **works** that I do shall he do also; and greater **works** that these shall he do, because I go to the Father."

1st Peter 2:12 (NASB)
(12) Keep your behavior excellent among the Gentiles, so that in the thing in which they slander you as evildoers, they may on account of your good deeds (*works*), as they observe them (*the works*), glorify God in the day of visitation.

Matthew 7:22-23 (NASB)
(22) "Many will say to Me on that day, 'LORD, LORD,
did we not prophesy in Your name, and in Your name
cast out demons, and in Your name perform many miracles?'"
(23) "And then I will declare to them, '**I never knew you,
DEPART FROM ME, YOU WHO PRACTICE LAWLESSNESS.**'" (sinful *works*)

Revelation 14:12 (KJV)
(12) Here is the patience of the Saints: here *are* they that
keep the Commandments of God (*works*), and the faith of Jesus.

Revelation 20:12-13 (KJV)
(12) And I saw the dead, small and great, stand before God; and the books were opened: and another was opened, which is the book of life: and the dead were judged out of those things which were written in the books, according to their **works**.
(13) And the sea gave up the dead which were in it; and death and hell delivered up the dead which were in them: and they were judged every man according to their **works**.

Revelation 22:12-14 **(KJV)**
(12) And, behold, I come quickly; and my reward is with me, to give every man **according as his WORK** shall be.
(13) I am Alpha and Omega, the beginning and the end, the first and the last.
(14) Blessed are they that do **HIS COMMANDMENTS** (*works*), that they may have right to the tree of life, and may enter in through the gates into **THE CITY**.

1 Samuel 15:22 (KJV)
22 And Samuel said, Hath the Lord as great delight in burnt offerings and sacrifices, as in

obeying the voice of the Lord?

Behold, **to obey is better than sacrifice**, and to hearken than the fat of rams.

The Law of Sin and Death

One of the reoccurring themes, which seems to permeate many of the sermons throughout most of Christianity, is that Jesus has delivered us from **"The Law of Sin and Death"**. They claim, we are not bound by **The Laws** of the Old Testament anymore. Would this be an accurate, or inaccurate, assessment of what Paul was trying to convey to the Congregation in Rome, to whom he was writing?

Romans 8:2-4 (NIV)
(2) because through Christ Jesus **The Law of the Spirit of Life** set me **FREE** from **The Law of Sin and Death**.
(3) For what The Law was powerless to do in that it was weakened by the sinful nature, God did by sending His own Son in the likeness of sinful man to be a sin offering. And so, he condemned sin in sinful man,
(4) in order that the righteous requirements of The Law might be fully met in us, who do not live according to the sinful nature but according to the Spirit.

Here we see that Paul is showing a dichotomy, between **The Law of the Spirit of Life** on one side and **The Law of Sin and Death** on the other. Paul is trying to convey how his own sinful nature had weakened and rendered The Law powerless. Which Law? Is it **The Law of the Spirit of Life** or **The Law of Sin and Death**? Paul concludes by talking about those who **do not** live according to the sinful nature, but according to the Spirit (*of Life*). Perhaps Paul, in his own way, is trying to remind the Church in Rome of what God had said in The Torah (*the first Five Books of the Old Testament*).

Deuteronomy 30:19-20 (NIV)
(19) This day I call heaven and earth as witnesses against you that **I have set before you life and death, blessings and curses. Now choose life,** so that you and your children may live
(20) and that you may **love** the Lord your God, listen to his voice, and hold fast to him. For the Lord is your life, and he will give you many years in the land he swore to give to your fathers, to Abraham, Isaac and Jacob.

It appears that Paul in his own way is trying to explain, in his letter to the Romans, that because of his own sinful nature he, in the past, had chosen sin, death and curses. But no longer! He had now made the choice to no longer live according to his old sinful nature. But now he had chosen to live according to the Spirit (*of Obedience*) and in doing so he had chosen **The Law of Life** and **Blessings**.

Matthew 19:17 (NIV)
(17) "Why do you ask me about what is good?" Jesus replied. "There is only One who is good. If you want to enter Life, **obey THE COMMANDMENTS.**"

Blessings and **Life** are the essence of **The Law of the Spirit of Life**, which comes into play through the observance and the keeping of, GOD'S COMMANDMENTS! **Curses and death** are at the very core of **The Law of Sin and Death**, which comes into play, when you **FREE** yourself from the observance and the keeping of, **GOD'S COMMANDMENTS and LAWS of LIFE and BLESSINGS!**

Paul *and* The LAW!

Romans 2:12-13

(NIV)
(12) All who sin apart from the LAW will also perish apart from the LAW, and all who sin under the Law will be judged by the LAW.
(13) For it is not those who hear the LAW who are righteous in God's sight, but it is those who **obey** the LAW who will be declared righteous.

(NASB)
(12) For all who have sinned without the LAW will also perish without the LAW; and all who have sinned under the LAW will be judged by the LAW;
(13) for not the hearers of the LAW are just before God, but the **doers** of the LAW will be justified.

Romans 3:31

(NIV)
(31) Do we, then, nullify the LAW by this faith? Not at all*!* Rather, we **uphold** the LAW.

(NASB)
(31) Do we then nullify the LAW through faith? May it never be! On the contrary, we **establish** the LAW.

Romans 7:12

(NIV)
(12) So then, the LAW is holy, and the commandment is **holy**, **righteous** and **good**.

(NASB)
(12) So then, the LAW is holy, and the commandment is **holy** and **righteous** and **good**.

Romans 7:22

(NIV)
(22) For in **my inner being** I delight in **God's LAW**;

(NASB)
(22) For I joyfully concur with the LAW **of God** in the **inner man**,

Romans 8:6-8

(NIV)
(6) The mind of sinful man is death, but the mind controlled by the Spirit is life and peace;
(7) the sinful mind is hostile to God. It does not submit to **God's LAW**, nor can it do so.
(8) Those controlled by the sinful nature cannot please God.

(NASB)
(6) For the mind set on the flesh is death, but the mind set on the Spirit is life and peace,
(7) because the mind set on the flesh is hostile toward God; for it does not subject itself to the LAW **of God**, for it is not even able to do so;
(8) and those who are in the flesh cannot please God.

1 Corinthians 7:19

(NASB)
(19) Circumcision is nothing, and uncircumcision is nothing, but what matters is the **keeping** of THE COMMANDMENTS OF GOD.

(NIV)
(19) Circumcision is nothing and uncircumcision is nothing. **Keeping GOD'S COMMANDS** is what counts.

1 Timothy 1:8

(NASB)
(8) But we know that the LAW **is good**, if one uses it lawfully,

(NIV)
(8) We know that the LAW **is good** if one uses it proper.

Words of Paul

Many times, people have a tendency to base much of their theology on the words of Paul alone. In doing so, often they will overlook the rest of the Scriptures. Thinking that their beliefs are correct and biblical.

But this raises an important question?

>If **Almighty GOD** in his word says one thing.

>With **GOD's Prophets** saying the same thing.

>Plus, **Words of Jesus** saying the same thing.

>Yet, the words of Paul, are <u>**appearing**</u> to be saying something else?

You should follow the words of **GOD**, **His Prophets** and **Jesus**?

And study to find out why there is an <u>**apparent**</u> contradiction, in the words of Paul?

>2 Peter 3:15-16 (NIV)
>**15** Bear in mind that our Lord's patience means salvation, just as our dear brother Paul also wrote you with the wisdom that God gave him.
>**16** He writes the same way in all his letters, speaking in them of these matters. His letters contain
>
>><u>**some things that are hard to understand**</u>,
>><u>**which ignorant and unstable people distort**</u>,
>><u>**as they do the other Scriptures,**</u>
>><u>**to their own destruction**</u>.

You should follow the words of **GOD**, **His Prophets** and **Jesus**? Even <u>**if**</u> it <u>**appears,**</u> that Paul may be saying something else**?**

If you put Paul's words first, instead of the words of **GOD** and **Jesus.**

Then, whether you realize it or not.

You are actually elevating Paul and his words, up to a level, that is <u>above</u> and <u>more important</u> (*in your mind*) <u>**than GOD**</u>, as well as <u>**more important**</u> than **GOD's Son**, **Jesus**!

Let Everything Be Established

Matthew 18:16 (NKJV)
¹⁶ But if he will not hear, take with you one **or two** more, that 'by the mouth of **two or three** witnesses every word may be established.'

2 Corinthians 13:1 (NKJV)
¹ This *will be* the third *time* I am coming to you. "By the mouth of **two or three** witnesses every word shall be established."

Hebrews 10:28 (NKJV)
²⁸ Anyone who has rejected Moses' law dies without mercy on *the testimony of* **two or three** witnesses.

Deuteronomy 17:6 (NKJV)
⁶ Whoever is deserving of death shall be put to death on the testimony of **two or three** witnesses; he shall **not** be put to death on the testimony of **one** witness.

Deuteronomy 19:15 (NKJV)
¹⁵ "One witness shall not rise against a man concerning any iniquity or any sin that he commits; by the mouth of **two or three** witnesses the matter shall be established.

John 8:17 (NKJV)
¹⁷ It is also written in your law that the testimony of **two men** is true.

1 Timothy 5:19 (NKJV)
¹⁹ Do not receive an accusation against an elder except from **two or three** witnesses.

Hebrews 10:28 (NKJV)
²⁸ Anyone who has rejected Moses' law dies without mercy on *the testimony of* **two or three** witnesses.

The Writings of Paul

Romans, 1 Corinthians, 2 Corinthians, Galatians, Ephesians, Philippians, Colossians, 1 Thessalonians 2 Thessalonians, 1 Timothy, 2 Timothy, Titus, Philemon and Hebrews

Other New Testament Writings

Matthew, Mark, Luke, John, James, 1 Peter, 2 Peter 1 John, 2 John, 3 John, Jude and Revelations

Old Testament Text

Genises through Malachi

So, using the above Scriptural examples. In order to establish any Theological Doctrine, we should have at least **two** and preferably **three or more**, Scriptural witnesses before we can establish any point of Doctrine. Even though you may have several examples from the writings of Paul. Paul can be only **one** of the witnesses. The others must come from either "Other New Testament Writings" and/or "The Old Testament Text". Because we need to have at the very least, **two or three** witnesses. Preferably, **even more**, before establishing **any** Doctrine.

www.ingramcontent.com/pod-product-compliance
Lightning Source LLC
Chambersburg PA
CBHW080839230426

43665CB00021B/2887